101 LASAGNAS
& OTHER LAYERED
CASSEROLES

101 LASAGNAS

& Other Layered Casseroles

JULIA RUTLAND

TILLER PRESS

NEW YORK LONDON TORONTO SYDNEY NEW DELHI

TILLER PRESS

An Imprint of Simon & Schuster, Inc.
1230 Avenue of the Americas
New York, NY 10020

First Tiller Press trade paperback edition December 2020

TILLER PRESS and colophon are trademarks of Simon & Schuster, Inc.

For information about special discounts for bulk purchases, please contact
Simon & Schuster Special Sales at 1-866-506-1949 or business@simonandschuster.com.

The Simon & Schuster Speakers Bureau can bring authors to your live event.
For more information or to book an event, contact the Simon & Schuster Speakers Bureau
at 1-866-248-3049 or visit our website at www.simonspeakers.com.

Cover and interior design by Matt Ryan
Photography produced by Blueline Creative Group LLC
Visit: www.bluelinecreativegroup.com
Produced by Katherine Cobbs
Photography by Becky Luigart-Stayner
Food Styling by Torie Cox
Prop Styling by Claire Spollen
Food Styling Assistance by Gordon Sawyer

Manufactured in the United States of America

1 3 5 7 9 10 8 6 4 2

Library of Congress Cataloging-in-Publication Data
Names: Rutland, Julia Dowling, author.
Title: 101 lasagnas & other layered casseroles / by Julia Rutland.
Other titles: 101 lasagnas and other layered casseroles
Description: New York : Tiller Press, 2020. | Includes index.
Identifiers: LCCN 2020031212 (print) | LCCN 2020031213 (ebook) |
ISBN 9781982163211 (paperback) | ISBN 9781982163228 (ebook)
Subjects: LCSH: Cooking (Pasta) | Cooking, Italian. | International cooking. | LCGFT: Cookbooks.
Classification: LCC TX809.M17 R88 2020 (print) | LCC TX809.M17 (ebook) | DDC 641.5945—dc23
LC record available at https://lccn.loc.gov/2020031212
LC ebook record available at https://lccn.loc.gov/2020031213

ISBN 978-1-9821-6321-1
ISBN 978-1-9821-6322-8 (ebook)

TABLE OF CONTENTS

Filling and satisfying, lasagnas make the ideal comfort-food meal.

These hearty casseroles fill your kitchen with tempting aromas, making mouths water and stomachs rumble. While many can be assembled on the fly, multilayered lasagnas with slow-cooked sauces and made-from-scratch fillings have flavors that prove they are worth any wait.

There is a great deal of emotional satisfaction in serving and eating lasagna, and the effort of their preparation is not lost on contented family and friends. Well-blended ingredients served piping hot nourish the body, but a home-cooked meal prepared with love feeds the soul as well.

Please enjoy this collection of lasagna casseroles that run the gamut from classic to extraordinary.

Lasagna 101

If you've never made a lasagna before, don't fear! Read these tips to ensure success. If you are a kitchen veteran, skim the tips as a refresher. I encourage you to try new flavors in new recipes—maybe you'll find your new signature dinner!

Baking & Casserole Dishes vs. Baking Pans

GLASS BAKEWARE, such as a glass or ceramic baking or casserole dish, conducts heat poorly so it heats up slowly. However, once it is hot, the dish distributes heat more evenly and consistently.

BAKING DISHES dissipate heat more slowly than metal, meaning lasagnas or other casseroles will stay hot longer when removed from the oven.

IF USING GLASS OR CERAMIC BAKING DISHES, some cooking experts recommend reducing the oven temperature by 25°F and shortening the cook time to avoid overbrowning. Personally, I find this to be true with baked goods like cakes and desserts, but less an issue with lasagnas and other savory casseroles.

BAKING DISHES ARE OFTEN MORE ATTRACTIVE than metal pans and can go from oven to table.

METAL BAKEWARE, such as baking pans, are able to withstand high temperatures like those used for broiling.

METAL BAKING PANS WILL BROWN FOODS FASTER and crisp the edges of the lasagna.

A METAL BAKING PAN CAN BE TRANSFERRED from the refrigerator to the oven without risk of breaking, like glass or ceramic dishes might.

CAST-IRON OR ALUMINUM BAKING PANS may react with acidic foods, adding a metallic taste or tinting the food an unappetizing color.

CONSIDER ENAMELED CAST IRON: it is relatively nonstick and doesn't react with acidic foods. (And the colorful interior/exterior are pretty enough for company!)

STANDARD VS. DEEP DISHES: Standard baking dishes are about two inches deep, while deep dishes are three or more inches deep. Most of the lasagna recipes in this book are meant for standard baking dishes or pans, but I've included a few hearty ones that will require deep sides to contain all the ingredients, especially while the lasagna is hot and bubbling in the oven. You can always bake a lasagna in a deep-dish container (the top might not brown as much, but otherwise it will be fine), but it's risky to use an undersized dish, since the overflow will burn on the oven floor. If there isn't at least half an inch of rim around the top once the lasagna is assembled, place the dish on a foil-lined baking sheet to catch spills.

Traditional Boiled Noodles

SALT THE WATER! Pasta is pretty bland on its own, and cooking the noodles in salted water infuses them with flavor. I use between one and two tablespoons of kosher salt for a big pot of water. I use kosher salt for pasta water because my fine sea salt, which I use for my recipes, is a bit gourmet and a lot more expensive. If you only have regular fine salt, use one to two teaspoons.

AVOID OVERCOOKING TRADITIONALLY BOILED LASAGNA NOODLES so they don't become mushy or torn apart. If unsure, err on the side of undercooking them since they will be cooked a second time after they are assembled into a lasagna.

AFTER DRAINING THE NOODLES, rinse them in cold water to avoid burning your fingers. Pasta purists don't rinse noodles because the starch on the surface helps sauces stick. I appreciate that technique, but I reserve that for dishes where I'm not manhandling boiling-hot noodles.

IF YOU LEAVE THE NOODLES IN A COLANDER for more than five or ten minutes, drizzle a small amount of olive oil on them and toss gently. This helps keep the noodles from sticking together. If you find noodles glued together in the colander, sigh loudly, and then rinse them in water until you can gently pry them apart. Don't fret over torn noodles; piece them together on the bottom layer.

IF COOKED NOODLES STAY OUT LONGER THAN THIRTY MINUTES, lay them out on a lightly greased sheet pan and cover with plastic wrap so they do not dry out and become brittle. This is the ideal way to treat lasagna noodles, but lazy cooks do not have to worry about the kitchen police if you skip this step. The resulting dish will taste just as yummy!

Specialty Lasagna Noodles

WHOLE-WHEAT LASAGNA, or any whole-grain pasta, can get mushy if overcooked. Watch carefully when boiling, and drain a minute or two early since the pasta will get cooked again when baked into a lasagna.

OVEN-READY NOODLES are thinner, wider, and shorter than traditional boiled lasagna noodles. If you have a gap larger than half an inch, you may want to break another noodle into pieces to fill in the space. Unless I know there is a lot of sauce or liquid in the lasagna, I don't overlap these noodles. The overlapped parts may not absorb enough liquid and remain tough. To make sure oven-ready noodles have cooked completely, stick a knife in the center to check for tenderness. If you meet resistance, keep cooking the lasagna.

COMMONLY FOUND GLUTEN-FREE LASAGNA NOODLES are usually a mix of corn and rice. If you want to avoid corn, look for lasagna sheets made from lentils. Gluten-free noodles are considered oven-ready, meaning there's no need to boil them before assembling the lasagna. Like wheat versions of oven-ready noodles, the gluten-free versions are smaller, and you may want to break some to cover the pan.

KETO NOODLES: These noodles go beyond gluten-free to exclude all grains in order to reduce carbs. Some brands use hearts of palm and are available at well-stocked grocery stores or through online specialty stores. These tend to be smaller than most other noodles and are notably more expensive.

Meat

HEARTY, PROTEIN-HEAVY LASAGNAS usually feature some type of ground meat as a base. There are many grades of ground beef, and you can use your favorite. Mixing some ground pork or sausage with the beef enhances its flavor. If you don't use a lean pork sausage, drain away any excess oil before adding the tomato product or any remaining ingredients.

OTHER CUTS OF BEEF CAN BE USED, but pieces should be bite-size or smaller to distribute evenly across a lasagna layer.

GROUND TURKEY OR CHICKEN are lower-fat options that can easily be substituted. These are generally so lean that they will require a tablespoon or so of olive oil to help them brown in the skillet without burning.

SLICED, CHOPPED, OR SHREDDED CHICKEN can be cooked with any method, but the best flavor comes from rotisserie or grilled chicken. Use light or dark meat as you wish. Leftover chicken can be shredded and measured into freezer-storage bags for use in future lasagnas.

MEATLESS OR VEGETARIAN MEAT CRUMBLES don't require any browning, but their bland flavor will benefit from being sautéed with aromatics like onion, garlic, and herbs. They are extremely lean and need oil to keep them from sticking to the pan.

Cheese

MOZZARELLA: This is probably the most commonly used cheese in my and millions of other lasagna recipes. Shredding cheese from blocks just prior to assembling the lasagna is, no question, the ideal method. A hand grater will give you a good workout, so consider the grating attachments of a food processor. That said, packaged shredded cheese is a convenience many people use. Go ahead and buy them—no judgment here. But remember that packaged shredded or grated cheese contains a bit of starch that keeps the pieces from sticking together, so these products don't have the same creamy meltability.

FRESH MOZZARELLA: Fresh mozzarella is an amazing fresh cheese—its cousin, Burrata cheese, is sublime. In a lasagna, however, the fresh, delicate flavor can get lost in all the tomato-pasta-veggie concoctions. Fresh mozzarella has more moisture, with a tender texture compared to a drier, more rubbery packaged brick mozzarella. It's more challenging to shred, but you can cut it into tiny pieces and scatter it among the lasagna layers. More often I use fresh mozzarella on the top of lasagnas where its delicate texture and mild flavor can be appreciated, especially if the top of the lasagna is sprinkled with chopped fresh basil.

PARMESAN, ROMANO, AND OTHER HARD CHEESES: These firmly pressed and dry types of cheese have loads of umami and also add salty flavor to lasagnas. In this book, I default to generic Parmesan since it's most readily available and less expensive than Parmigiano-Reggiano, Pecorino Romano, and Grana Padano. I tend to save the fine cheese for snacks and salads since mixing and baking with pounds of other ingredients tends to dilute the nuances that make those outstanding cheeses noteworthy. Generic and affordable Parmesan brands are often softer than their well-aged spendy counterparts, making them easier to grate by hand or with a food processor.

OTHER: Asiago, Gruyère, Provolone, Cheddar, Gouda, Swiss, Monterey Jack, Pepper Jack, Blue, Feta, Goat . . . and the list goes on! Experiment by substituting your favorite cheese in these recipes. High-moisture cheeses melt faster while crumbly, drier cheeses (such as those made from sheep's milk like Feta and Manchego) won't always melt to a smooth texture in white sauces, so don't fret trying to incorporate them. Some cheeses are pretty oily (like Gruyère), so consider using a blend to avoid puddling.

Ricotta & Ricotta-Blend Fillings

RICOTTA: Many lasagna recipes include one or more layers of ricotta cheese. People will fall into three camps: lasagna must include ricotta, must never include ricotta, and it doesn't matter as long as it tastes good! I will not attempt to change your mind. Many of the recipes in this book contain ricotta because I like it and I also want to bump up the protein content, especially in the vegetarian dishes. If you really dislike it, just skip that filling and assemble without it.

RICOTTA IS A SIMPLE CHEESE that can be made quickly and with just three ingredients— milk, salt, and an acid such as lemon juice or vinegar. I always prefer the flavor of fresh-made ricotta, but I tested with many different grocery-store brands for ease and consistency. Look at the label—some contain a lot of thickeners—and choose a brand with the fewest ingredients. I prefer whole-milk ricotta but have used the lower-fat versions with similar results. Some brands are thick; others a bit watery. If your ricotta is very thin, you could strain it through coffee filters to thicken it up (you shouldn't have to do that, however; buy another brand next time). In most recipes, I add an egg to help bind the filling ingredients.

COTTAGE CHEESE CAN SUBSTITUTE FOR RICOTTA in many recipes. For the closest approximation, use small curd or process large-curd cottage cheese in a food processor for a few seconds. Large curd is an interesting option in lasagna layers because of its chewy texture. Before using, drain any excess liquid from the top.

Tomato, Pasta, Marinara, Pizza & Other Red Sauces

A HOMEMADE SAUCE WILL ALMOST ALWAYS WIN a taste-test contest against jarred versions, but sometimes you'll want to take a shortcut and use a prepared sauce from the market. In this collection of recipes, you can pick your favorite brand and flavor. Sometimes the tomato sauce is just a backdrop to some interesting fillings and vegetable combinations, so you'll want a nondescript sauce that won't compete.

A COMMON JAR SIZE for marinara or pasta sauce is twenty-four ounces. This works out to be somewhere between two and three quarters to three cups. If you make or buy sauce in bulk, you can measure out three cups and use it for any of the recipes indicating a twenty-four-ounce jar size.

TOMATO SAUCE IS SMOOTH, while pasta and marinara sauces may have larger pieces of tomatoes and other vegetables. You can substitute one for another, but tomato sauce may taste plain, depending if seasonings were added. Authentic sauce purists favor San Marzano tomato sauces. The name refers to the type of Roma tomato, not how it was processed.

CRUSHED TOMATOES will be thinner and less smooth than tomato sauce. I tend to use it in sauces that are cooked down a bit so the excess water evaporates. Cooking a sauce longer tends to add flavor.

PUREED TOMATOES are thicker than crushed, and a bit smoother.

TOMATO PASTE is thick and concentrated. It adds a rich tomato flavor when added to sauces.

Béchamel, Alfredo, Cheese & Other White Sauces

DAIRY-BASED SAUCES help soften the acidity in tomato-based sauces and are included in a great many of the lasagnas in this book. Like the ricotta debate, some people insist béchamel or other white sauce be included in the lasagna layers while some oppose it. It's not as easy to skip the white sauce (like you can skip ricotta fillings) in these recipes since sometimes it's the only sauce or critical moisture element to ensure tender noodles.

BÉCHAMEL in its basic form is simply flour, butter, and milk. But that trio is a bit bland, so I add aromatics like onion and garlic with a bit of salt and nutmeg to punch up the flavor. A roux is made with flour and butter (or sometimes olive oil) and is cooked for at least a minute to get rid of the raw flour taste. Additional cooking darkens the roux and gives it a nuttier flavor.

SINCE CHEESE IS A NATURAL COMPANION TO LASAGNAS, I'll add cheese to many of the white sauces to thicken them, as well as to add additional flavor. Sometimes I'll use broth in the white sauce (called a velouté), but I tend to take liberties and add some cream, half and half, or other dairy to add richness.

ALFREDO SAUCE is traditionally made with heavy cream, butter, and Parmesan cheese. When it breaks, the butter will separate from the rest of the ingredients, leaving it a little curdled. This happens with high heat and often when reheating leftovers. A lasagna sauce is cooked twice— once in a saucepan or skillet and the second time in the oven. To ensure a smooth sauce, I like to start with a roux, like the béchamel sauce, but then add Parmesan. It has the flavor of an Alfredo with more stability.

SINCE I'M USUALLY ADDING OTHER INGREDIENTS, I'll make most of my white sauces from scratch. Packaged Alfredo sauces often contain sugar or corn syrup, as well as thickening agents and preservatives to make them shelf stable. When buying, read the label, especially if you are avoiding sugar and gluten in your diet.

Layering

THE WAY THE LASAGNA IS LAYERED is less important than the detailed directions may lead you to believe. If you mix up a layer, no worries. Just make sure you don't double up the pasta noodles, especially the oven-ready types. If stacked too tightly, they may not absorb enough liquid to become tender.

SPOON HALF A CUP OR MORE SAUCE in the bottom of the lightly greased dish or pan before adding the first layer of noodles. This keeps the bottom layer of pasta from sticking to the pan.

MAKE SURE THE FINAL LAYER OF NOODLES is completely covered with a sauce or another ingredient. Even if the lasagna is covered in foil while baking, any uncovered noodles may become too tough to eat.

Covered vs. Uncovered

COVERING THE LASAGNA while baking ensures the ingredients have cooked completely before the top is golden brown. This is critical with oven-ready noodles since they depend on moisture to rehydrate and soften.

I INCLUDED A FEW RECIPES THAT SUGGEST BAKING UNCOVERED. These recipes use vegetables that tend to release a lot of water when cooked, and baking the lasagna uncovered helps evaporate the excess moisture.

ALWAYS UNCOVER FOR THE LAST TEN TO TWENTY MINUTES to get a lovely golden-brown top. For extra browning (important to those of us who love dark, bubbly cheese), leave the lasagna in the oven and broil it for a few minutes until it reaches the color you like.

CHEESE STICKS TO FOIL. Cheese *really* sticks to foil. Nonstick foil offers the best results. If not available, spray foil liberally with cooking spray before covering so the topping doesn't end up on the foil instead of the lasagna. If that happens—and it happens to all of us at some time—simply scrape the cheese off the foil and dollop it on top of the lasagna. Just sprinkle a bunch of chopped herbs over the lasagna to hide the mess!

Rest

LASAGNAS OFTEN BENEFIT FROM A TEN- TO FIFTEEN-MINUTE REST before slicing, especially those with a lot of moist ingredients. The slight cooling helps keep the layers together, making them easy to serve. (Plus, you're not trying to eat a lava-hot dinner!)

IF YOU CUT INTO A LASAGNA and it appears a bit watery on the bottom, let it stand a few more minutes and cut another slice. The extra time allows the noodles to absorb more liquid. You can also sprinkle a few breadcrumbs or a fine grated hard cheese on the bottom of your plate.

HERE'S A TIP IF YOU LIKE TO POST YOUR DINNERS ONLINE: Hot lasagna can be messy and uncooperative when photographed—cut your hero serving when it's almost cold. The layers won't slip around, and you'll be able to see the fillings more clearly. If the cheesy topping looks too solid, heat it under the broiler for a minute to soften and shine it up.

MEAT

Lasagna Bolognese

Traditional Bolognese is a hearty meat sauce with some finely chopped veggies that are pretty well hidden but important to the flavor. Milk is added at the end to add silkiness to the sauce and to blunt the acidity of the tomatoes. The best flavor comes after a very long simmer, so be patient and you'll be rewarded with an amazing sauce.

SERVES 8 TO 10

BOLOGNESE SAUCE

- 2 tablespoons extra-virgin olive oil
- 4 ounces pancetta or bacon, chopped (about ½ cup)
- 1 onion, finely chopped
- 2 carrots, finely chopped
- 2 celery stalks, finely chopped
- 1 pound ground beef
- 1 pound ground pork, chicken, or turkey
- 3 garlic cloves, minced
- ¾ cup dry white wine
- 1 (28-ounce) can crushed tomatoes
- 1 cup beef stock or broth
- 2 tablespoons tomato paste
- ½ teaspoon fine sea salt
- ½ teaspoon freshly ground black pepper
- 1 cup whole milk

BASIC BÉCHAMEL SAUCE

- 4 tablespoons butter
- ¼ cup all-purpose flour
- 3 cups whole milk
- ½ teaspoon fine sea salt
- ¼ teaspoon freshly ground black pepper
- ½ teaspoon ground nutmeg

- 1 (16-ounce) package lasagna noodles
- 2 cups (8 ounces) shredded mozzarella cheese
- 2 cups (8 ounces) shredded or grated Parmesan cheese
- ¼ cup chopped fresh basil

MAKE THE BOLOGNESE SAUCE: Heat the oil in a soup pot over medium and add the pancetta. Cook, stirring occasionally, for 5 minutes until crispy. Add the onion, carrots, and celery. Cook, stirring occasionally, for 10 minutes until the vegetables are tender. Add the beef, pork, and garlic. Cook, stirring occasionally, for 10 minutes until the meat is browned and crumbly. Add the wine. Cook for 3 to 5 minutes until the liquid evaporates. Stir in the tomatoes, stock, tomato paste, salt, and pepper. Bring the mixture to a boil and reduce the heat to low. Simmer, with the lid partially covered, for 2 to 3 hours. (Make sure the heat remains low enough so the liquid doesn't completely evaporate.) Add the milk, stirring until well blended.

PREHEAT THE OVEN to 350°F. Lightly grease a 13 x 9-inch deep baking dish.

MAKE THE BASIC BÉCHAMEL SAUCE: Melt the butter in a large skillet over medium-high heat. Whisk in the flour. Cook, stirring constantly, for 1 minute. Whisk in the milk, salt, black pepper, and nutmeg. Cook, stirring frequently, for 5 minutes until thickened.

COOK THE LASAGNA NOODLES in boiling salted water according to the package directions. Drain, then rinse in cool water.

ASSEMBLE: Spread ½ cup of the béchamel sauce in the bottom of the prepared dish. Top with 5 noodles, overlapping slightly. Spread one-third of the Bolognese sauce, one-third of the béchamel sauce, and one-third each of the mozzarella and Parmesan. Repeat twice in this order: noodles, Bolognese sauce, béchamel sauce, mozzarella, and Parmesan.

COVER AND BAKE for 30 minutes. Uncover and broil for 3 minutes, if desired, until golden brown and bubbly. Let stand for 15 minutes before serving. Sprinkle with the basil.

Deep-Dish Sausage & Spinach Lasagna

Fans of traditional deep-dish lasagna should keep this one on rotation. Canned tomatoes can be bland, so I add a bit of balsamic vinegar, brown sugar, and smoked paprika to the sauce toward the end of cooking.

SERVES 10

SMOKY SAUSAGE SAUCE

- 1 tablespoon extra-virgin olive oil
- 1 pound Italian link sausage, casings removed
- 1 onion, chopped
- 3 garlic cloves, chopped
- 1 tablespoon Italian seasoning
- 2 (28-ounce) cans crushed tomatoes with basil
- 2 tablespoons balsamic vinegar
- 1 tablespoon light or dark brown sugar
- 1 teaspoon smoked paprika, optional

SPINACH-RICOTTA FILLING

- 1½ cups ricotta cheese
- 1 (16-ounce) package frozen leaf spinach, thawed and drained
- 1 large egg
- ½ teaspoon fine sea salt
- ¼ teaspoon freshly ground black pepper

- 12 lasagna noodles
- 2 cups (8 ounces) shredded mozzarella cheese
- ½ cup (2 ounces) shredded or grated Parmesan cheese

PREHEAT THE OVEN to 350°F. Lightly grease a deep 13 x 9-inch lasagna pan or baking dish.

MAKE THE SMOKY SAUSAGE SAUCE: Heat the oil in a large, deep skillet over medium-high. Add the sausage, onion, garlic, and Italian seasoning. Cook, stirring frequently, for 7 minutes or until the sausage is cooked and crumbly and the onion is tender. Stir in the crushed tomatoes. Cook, stirring occasionally, for 20 to 30 minutes. Stir in the vinegar, brown sugar, and paprika. Cook, stirring occasionally, for 10 minutes.

MAKE THE SPINACH-RICOTTA FILLING: Stir together the ricotta cheese, spinach, egg, salt, and pepper in a large bowl. Set aside.

COOK THE LASAGNA NOODLES in salted boiling water according to the package directions. Drain, then rinse with cool water.

ASSEMBLE: Spoon 1½ cups of the sauce into the bottom of the pan. Top with 4 noodles, overlapping slightly. Spread half the spinach mixture over the noodles and top with one-third of the sauce. Repeat with 4 noodles, remaining spinach, and one-third of the remaining sauce. Top with the remaining 4 noodles and remaining sauce. Sprinkle the top evenly with the mozzarella and Parmesan.

COVER AND BAKE for 30 minutes. Uncover and bake for 20 minutes until the lasagna is bubbly and the top is golden brown. Let stand for 10 minutes before serving.

MEAT

Meatloaf Lasagna

Worcestershire sauce is the key ingredient that makes this beef mixture taste like a traditional meatloaf. The top layer of the meat tends to shrink a little when cooked, but it won't show since the loaf is served upside down. You can use gluten-free noodles, but you may need to add a piece of another noodle to cover the filling since they tend to be shorter than wheat noodles.

〜〜〜〜〜〜〜〜〜 **SERVES 4 TO 6** 〜〜〜〜〜〜〜〜〜

RICOTTA FILLING

1 (15-ounce) container ricotta cheese

½ cup (2 ounces) shredded mozzarella cheese

¼ cup (1 ounce) shredded or grated Parmesan cheese

1 large egg

¼ teaspoon fine sea salt

MEATLOAF MIXTURE

½ pound lean ground beef

½ pound lean ground pork or pork sausage

2 tablespoons finely chopped onion

1 garlic clove, minced

1 large egg

1½ teaspoons Worcestershire sauce

¾ teaspoon fine sea salt

¼ teaspoon freshly ground black pepper

½ cup dried breadcrumbs

⅓ cup chopped fresh Italian parsley

4 to 6 oven-ready lasagna noodles

1 cup pasta or marinara sauce

1 tablespoon light or dark brown sugar

1 teaspoon sriracha or hot sauce

½ cup (2 ounces) shredded mozzarella cheese

¼ cup (1 ounce) shredded or grated Parmesan cheese

PREHEAT THE OVEN to 350°F. Line a 9 x 5-inch loaf pan with nonstick aluminum foil.

MAKE THE RICOTTA FILLING: Combine the ricotta, mozzarella, Parmesan, egg, and salt in a bowl.

MAKE THE MEATLOAF MIXTURE: Combine the ground beef, ground pork, onion, garlic, egg, Worcestershire sauce, salt, pepper, breadcrumbs, and parsley in a large bowl. With wet hands, blend together until thoroughly mixed.

ASSEMBLE: Press half the beef mixture into the bottom of the loaf pan. Top with a lasagna noodle, breaking a piece off another to create a single layer in the pan. Spread with ½ cup of the ricotta filling. Repeat three more times with the lasagna noodles and ricotta filling. Press the remaining beef mixture in a flat layer over the ricotta cheese.

BAKE, UNCOVERED, for 45 minutes. Meanwhile, combine the pasta sauce, brown sugar, and sriracha sauce in a small bowl.

TURN THE PAN upside down on a foil-lined baking sheet. Remove the foil from the top. Spoon the pasta sauce mixture over the top and sprinkle with the mozzarella and Parmesan cheese. Broil for 3 to 5 minutes, or until the cheese is golden brown and bubbly. Let stand for 10 minutes before serving.

Spaghetti Lasagna

Use any cooked spaghetti or other noodle in this hearty casserole.
Red lentil, black bean, vegetable-infused, or whole-grain pasta
add a new level of flavor and nutrition.

〜〜〜〜〜〜〜〜〜 **SERVES 8** 〜〜〜〜〜〜〜〜〜

ITALIAN MEAT SAUCE

2 tablespoons extra-virgin olive oil

1 onion, chopped

1 pound ground beef

½ pound spicy Italian sausage

3 garlic cloves, minced

2 (24-ounce) jars pasta or marinara sauce

2 tablespoons red wine

RICOTTA FILLING

1 (15-ounce) container ricotta cheese

1 large egg

1 cup (4 ounces) shredded mozzarella cheese

½ cup (2 ounces) shredded or grated Parmesan cheese

¼ teaspoon fine sea salt

¼ teaspoon freshly ground black pepper

1 (16-ounce) package spaghetti

2 cups (8 ounces) shredded mozzarella cheese

¼ cup chopped fresh Italian parsley

PREHEAT THE OVEN to 350°F. Lightly grease a 13 x 9-inch deep baking dish.

MAKE THE ITALIAN MEAT SAUCE: Heat the olive oil in a large pot over medium-high. Add the onion and cook, stirring occasionally, for 5 minutes. Add the beef, sausage, and garlic. Cook, stirring occasionally, for 10 minutes until the meat is browned and crumbly. Stir in the pasta sauce and the wine.

MAKE THE RICOTTA FILLING: Combine the ricotta, egg, mozzarella, Parmesan, salt, and pepper in a bowl.

COOK THE SPAGHETTI in boiling salted water according to the package directions. Drain and add to the meat sauce, tossing well.

ASSEMBLE: Spread half the spaghetti and sauce in the bottom of the prepared dish. Top with all of the ricotta filling. Top with the remaining spaghetti. Top evenly with the mozzarella cheese.

COVER AND BAKE for 30 minutes. Uncover and bake for 10 minutes until golden brown and bubbly. Let stand for 10 minutes before serving. Sprinkle with the parsley.

Microwave Lasagna for One

This simple lasagna makes an ideal dorm dinner or work lunch when all you have is a microwave to cook food. Make sure to use a microwave-safe glass or ceramic dish—no plastic because it might melt. Ricotta cheese on its own can be bland—jazz it up with pinch of salt, a little Italian seasoning blend, a dollop of pesto, or bit of chopped fresh basil.

SERVES 1

- 2 oven-ready or gluten-free lasagna noodles
- 1 cup pasta or marinara sauce
- ½ cup ricotta or small-curd cottage cheese
- 1 cooked beef hamburger patty or veggie burger patty, crumbled
- ½ cup (2 ounces) shredded Italian blend or mozzarella cheese

BREAK THE LASAGNA NOODLES in half crosswise (to create four square pieces) and soak them in warm water for 15 minutes until pliable.

ASSEMBLE: Spoon 2 tablespoons of the sauce in the bottom of a lightly greased microwave-safe baking dish or bowl. Top with a noodle piece, one-fourth of the ricotta, one-fourth of the burger, 1 tablespoon cheese, and one-fourth of the sauce. Repeat with remaining noodle pieces, ricotta, burger, cheese, and sauce. Sprinkle the remaining cheese on top.

COVER AND REFRIGERATE up to a day ahead.

MICROWAVE ON HIGH for 5 to 7 minutes until hot and bubbly. Let stand for 5 minutes before serving.

MEAT

Beefy Alfredo Lasagna for Two

Here's a full-flavored lasagna for people not interested in leftovers (well, not much—it's a generous portion). It's ideal for a cozy dinner for two and only needs a green salad on the side to round out the meal. If I'm using a prepared Alfredo sauce instead of homemade for small-scale lasagnas, I prefer the refrigerated brands since their small size means no opened jars in the fridge.

~~~~~~~~~~~~~~~~~~~~ SERVES 2 ~~~~~~~~~~~~~~~~~~~~

SMALL-BATCH MEAT SAUCE

- 1 tablespoon extra-virgin olive oil
- ½ sweet onion, finely chopped
- ½ to ¾ pound ground beef
- 2 garlic cloves, minced
- 1 teaspoon dried oregano
- ½ teaspoon fine sea salt
- ¼ cup red or white wine or beef broth
- 1 (28-ounce) can crushed tomatoes
- Pinch sugar

- 3 oven-ready lasagna noodles
- 1 (10-ounce) container refrigerated Alfredo sauce (about 1 cup)
- 1 cup (4 ounces) shredded Italian blend cheese

PREHEAT THE OVEN to 375°F. Lightly grease a 9 x 5-inch loaf pan.

MAKE THE SMALL-BATCH MEAT SAUCE: Heat the oil in a large saucepan over medium-high. Add the onion and cook, stirring frequently, for 3 minutes. Add the beef, garlic, oregano, and salt. Cook, stirring frequently, for 5 minutes until browned and crumbly. Stir in the wine. Cook, stirring frequently, for 3 minutes until the liquid evaporates. Stir in the tomatoes and sugar. Cook, stirring occasionally, for 15 to 30 minutes until thickened.

ASSEMBLE: Spread ½ cup meat sauce in the bottom of the prepared pan. Top with 1 noodle, one-third of the remaining meat sauce, one-third of the Alfredo sauce, and one-third of the cheese. Repeat twice in this order: noodle, meat sauce, Alfredo, and cheese.

COVER AND BAKE for 40 minutes. Uncover and bake for 10 minutes or broil for 3 minutes until golden brown and bubbly. Let stand for 10 minutes before serving.

MEAT

25

Make-Ahead Spinach Lasagna for a Crowd

This traditional lasagna includes some spinach to sneak in a little healthy veg. For ease, don't bother with thawing loose cut leaf frozen spinach, since it defrosts quickly. Frozen block-style spinach will need to thaw before using. For food safety, make sure the center of the casserole is at least 160°F, since a chilled casserole takes longer to cook. Use disposable pans that won't need to be returned, and cook on a baking sheet, since the pans are flexible. To travel, wrap the lasagna in a towel to keep warm and place on a cool baking pan to prevent burns.

SERVES 24

SPINACH-MEAT SAUCE
- 2 tablespoons extra-virgin olive oil
- 2 onions, chopped
- 2 pounds sweet or hot Italian sausage, casings removed
- 1 pound lean ground beef
- 6 garlic cloves, minced
- 1 tablespoon Italian seasoning blend
- ½ cup red wine (optional)
- 1 (16-ounce) package frozen cut leaf spinach (thawed or unthawed)
- 1 (66-ounce) jar of pasta or marinara sauce
- 2 beef bouillon cubes

BÉCHAMEL SAUCE
- 4 tablespoons butter
- ⅓ cup all-purpose flour
- 4 cups whole milk
- 1 teaspoon fine sea salt
- ¼ teaspoon ground nutmeg

RICOTTA FILLING
- 1 (32-ounce) container ricotta cheese
- 3 large eggs
- 2 cups (8 ounces) shredded mozzarella cheese
- 1 teaspoon fine sea salt
- ½ teaspoon freshly ground black pepper

- 2 (13½ x 9⅝-inch) disposable lasagna pans
- 2 (16-ounce) boxes oven-ready lasagna noodles
- 2 cups (8 ounces) shredded mozzarella cheese
- 1 cup (4 ounces) shredded or grated Parmesan cheese

MAKE THE SPINACH-MEAT SAUCE: Heat the olive in a large soup pot over medium. Add the onions and cook, stirring occasionally, for 5 minutes or until tender. Add the sausage, beef, garlic, and Italian seasoning. Cook, stirring occasionally, for 10 to 15 minutes until the meat is browned and crumbly. Stir in the wine, if using. Cook, stirring occasionally, for 5 minutes. Stir in the spinach, pasta sauce, and bouillon cubes. Cook, stirring occasionally, for 30 minutes.

MAKE THE BÉCHAMEL SAUCE: Melt the butter in a large skillet or saucepan over medium-high. Whisk in the flour and cook, stirring constantly, for 1 minute. Whisk in the milk, salt, and nutmeg. Cook, stirring frequently, for 10 minutes until thickened.

MAKE THE RICOTTA FILLING: Stir together the ricotta, eggs, mozzarella, salt, and pepper in a bowl.

ASSEMBLE: Lightly grease the lasagna pans. Spread ½ cup of the béchamel sauce in the bottom of each pan. Top with 4 or 5 noodles. Spread about 1 cup of the ricotta mixture over the noodles. Top with 1⅓ cups of the meat sauce. Repeat with remaining noodles, ricotta, and meat sauce. Spread half of the remaining béchamel sauce (about 1½ cups) over each lasagna. Sprinkle each evenly with the mozzarella and Parmesan cheese.

COVER AND REFRIGERATE up to a day ahead until ready to cook.

PREHEAT THE OVEN to 350°F. Place the lasagna on a baking sheet. Bake, covered, for 45 to 60 minutes until hot in the center. Uncover and bake for 15 minutes, or broil for 3 to 5 minutes, until golden brown and bubbly. Let stand for 15 minutes before serving.

Spicy Meatball Lasagna

It's not critical if the meatballs are of identical size, but they should be fairly similar for even cooking. When portioning out recipes like this, I divide the mixture in three even parts, then divide those into three. Then it's pretty easy to divide the smaller portions into four meatballs that are the same size.

〰〰〰 **SERVES 8** 〰〰〰

MEATBALLS

1 pound ground beef

1 pound spicy Italian sausage links, casings removed

⅓ cup Italian-seasoned panko or fine breadcrumbs

¼ cup (1 ounce) Parmesan cheese

¼ cup minced onion

2 teaspoons Italian seasoning

1 large egg

8 to 10 lasagna noodles

RICOTTA FILLING

1 (15-ounce) container ricotta cheese

1 large egg

⅓ cup chopped Italian parsley

½ teaspoon fine sea salt

½ teaspoon freshly ground black pepper

1 (24-ounce) jar pasta or marinara sauce

2 cups (8-ounces) shredded mozzarella cheese

PREHEAT THE OVEN to 375F°. Line two baking sheets with nonstick aluminum foil. Lightly grease a 13 x 9-inch baking dish.

MAKE THE MEATBALLS: Combine the beef, sausage, panko, Parmesan, onion, Italian seasoning, and egg in a large bowl, mixing with your hands until thoroughly blended. Shape the mixture into 36 meatballs, about 1½ inches in diameter. Bake for 20 minutes until cooked through. Set aside.

COOK THE LASAGNA NOODLES in boiling salted water according to the package directions. Drain, then rinse with cool water.

MAKE THE RICOTTA FILLING: Combine the ricotta, egg, parsley, salt, and pepper in a medium bowl. Set aside.

ASSEMBLE: Spread 1 cup of the pasta sauce on the bottom of prepared dish. Cover with 4 to 5 lasagna noodles. Spread the noodles with half the ricotta mixture, half the meatballs, 1 cup of sauce, and 1½ cups of mozzarella. Repeat with the remaining 4 to 5 noodles, half of the ricotta, half of the meatballs, sauce, and mozzarella cheese.

COVER AND BAKE for 40 minutes. Uncover and bake for 15 minutes until golden brown. Let stand for 15 minutes before slicing.

MEAT

Dutch Oven Stovetop Lasagna

Campers or outdoor cooks can have lasagna without using an oven by cooking it on a stovetop, outdoor grill, or even a campfire. If you prepare this inside, a simple Dutch oven or cassoulet dish works. Outside or on the grill requires a heavy-duty pot made of cast iron to avoid hot spots and to provide even heating.

~~~~~~ **SERVES 6** ~~~~~~

- 2 tablespoons extra-virgin olive oil
- 1 small onion, chopped
- 3 garlic cloves, minced
- ½ pound lean ground beef
- ½ pound uncooked spicy Italian sausage, casings removed
- 8 lasagna noodles, cracked into 2-inch pieces
- 1 (24-ounce) jar pasta or marinara sauce
- 1 cup ricotta or cottage cheese
- 1 cup (4 ounces) shredded mozzarella cheese
- 1 cup (4 ounces) shredded or grated Parmesan cheese
- ¼ cup chopped fresh basil or prepared pesto sauce

HEAT THE OIL in a large Dutch oven over medium. Add the onion and cook, stirring occasionally, for 5 minutes. Add the garlic, beef, and sausage and cook, stirring occasionally, for 10 minutes until the meat is browned and crumbly. Drain any excess oil, if necessary.

SPREAD THE BROKEN NOODLES evenly over the cooked meat and top with the pasta sauce and 1 cup water. (Do not stir the sauce into the noodles; they must be covered completely with the liquid.) Bring the mixture to a boil. Reduce the heat to low and cook, covered, for 40 minutes or until the noodles are tender.

STIR THE MIXTURE slightly, separating the noodles. Dollop the ricotta cheese around the top of the lasagna. Sprinkle with the mozzarella and Parmesan. Cover and cook for 15 minutes or until the cheese melts. Let stand for 10 minutes before serving. Sprinkle with fresh basil or drizzle with pesto.

Moussaka-Style Lasagna

Rich and comforting, this riff on the classic Greek casserole includes two layers of noodles that give it extra heft. Egg yolks are added to the béchamel sauce to tighten it up, making it easier to create even slices.

〜〜〜〜〜〜〜〜〜〜 **SERVES 8** 〜〜〜〜〜〜

1 eggplant

½ teaspoon fine sea salt

2 tablespoons extra-virgin olive oil

4 Yukon gold or 2 russet potatoes

MOUSSAKA MEAT SAUCE

1 tablespoon extra-virgin olive oil

1 onion, chopped

1 pound lean ground lamb or beef

2 garlic cloves, minced

1 teaspoon Italian seasoning

¾ teaspoon ground cinnamon

½ teaspoon fine sea salt

¼ teaspoon cayenne pepper

¼ teaspoon freshly ground black pepper

¼ cup red wine

1 (28-ounce) can crushed tomatoes

1 teaspoon sugar

YOGURT BÉCHAMEL SAUCE

2 tablespoons butter

2 tablespoons all-purpose flour

2 cups milk or half and half

1 (5.3-ounce) container plain Greek yogurt

¼ teaspoon fine sea salt

¼ teaspoon ground nutmeg

Small pinch ground cloves

3 large egg yolks

8 oven-ready lasagna noodles

½ cup (2 ounces) crumbled feta or shredded Parmesan cheese

PREHEAT THE OVEN to 425°F. Lightly grease an 8 x 8-inch baking dish. Place a wire cooling rack over a baking sheet.

PEEL THE EGGPLANT and slice it lengthwise ⅛ to ¼ inch thick. Sprinkle ½ teaspoon salt evenly over both sides. Place on a wire rack and let stand for 10 to 20 minutes. Blot dry with paper towels. Brush both sides evenly with olive oil. Bake for 10 minutes on each side until tender and browned along the edges. Remove from the oven, then reduce the heat to 350°F.

PEEL THE POTATOES and slice ¼ inch thick. Cook the potatoes in boiling salted water for 5 minutes, until just barely tender. Drain, then rinse in cool water. Set aside.

MAKE THE MOUSSAKA MEAT SAUCE: Heat the olive oil in a large skillet. Add the onion and cook, stirring frequently, for 5 minutes until tender. Add the meat and garlic. Cook, stirring frequently, until the meat is browned and crumbly. Stir in the Italian seasoning, cinnamon, salt, cayenne pepper, and black pepper. Add the wine and cook for 1 to 2 minutes until the liquid is reduced. Stir in the tomatoes and sugar. Cook, stirring frequently, until the sauce thickens.

MAKE THE YOGURT BÉCHAMEL: Melt the butter in a large skillet over medium-high. Whisk in the flour. Cook, stirring constantly, for 1 minute. Whisk in the milk. Cook, stirring frequently, for 5 minutes until the mixture thickens. Stir in the yogurt, salt, nutmeg, and cloves. Cool slightly and add the egg yolks, stirring until well blended.

ASSEMBLE: Arrange the potatoes on the bottom of the prepared baking dish. Top with half the meat sauce and 4 noodles, breaking to fit if necessary. Layer all of the eggplant over the noodles. Top with the remaining half of the meat sauce and remaining 4 noodles. Cover with all of the béchamel. Sprinkle with the feta or Parmesan cheese.

COVER AND BAKE for 40 minutes. If desired, uncover and broil for 3 minutes until golden brown. Let stand for 10 minutes before serving.

MEAT

31

Keto-Cabbage Lasagna

You will never miss the noodles in this highly seasoned and delicious dish. Cooking the cabbage leaves in salted water will help draw out moisture and tenderize the hearty leaves. The sauce needs to be thick since the cabbage will continue to release liquid when cooked.

~~~~~~~~~~ **SERVES 8** ~~~~~~~~~~

SPICY KETO MEAT SAUCE

- 2 tablespoons extra-virgin olive oil
- 1 onion, chopped
- 1 green bell pepper, chopped
- 3 garlic cloves, minced
- 1 pound ground beef
- ½ pound spicy Italian sausage, casings removed
- ¼ teaspoon smoked paprika or crushed red pepper flakes
- 1 tablespoon Italian seasoning
- 1 (28-ounce) can crushed tomatoes
- 2 small cubes beef bouillon, crushed

- 1 (2- to 2½-pound) head green cabbage

RICH COTTAGE CHEESE FILLING

- 1 (32-ounce) container cottage cheese or ricotta cheese
- 2 large eggs
- 1 cup (4 ounces) shredded mozzarella cheese
- 1 cup (4 ounces) shredded or grated Parmesan cheese
- ¼ cup chopped fresh basil
- ¼ teaspoon fine sea salt

- 1 cup (4 ounces) shredded mozzarella cheese
- 1 cup (4 ounces) shredded or grated Parmesan cheese

PREPARE THE SPICY KETO MEAT SAUCE: Heat the oil in a large skillet over medium-high. Add the onion and bell pepper and cook, stirring frequently, for 5 minutes until tender. Add the garlic, beef, sausage, paprika, and Italian seasoning. Cook, stirring occasionally, for 10 minutes until the meat is browned and crumbly. Add the crushed tomatoes and bouillon. Cook, stirring occasionally, for 20 minutes.

PREHEAT THE OVEN to 375°F. Lightly grease a 13 x 9-inch baking dish.

CUT THE CABBAGE in half and remove the core. Peel the leaves from the cabbage and cut away any hard, thick ribs. Cook in boiling salted water to cover for 5 minutes or until the leaves are tender. Drain well in a colander and then transfer to baking sheets to air dry.

MAKE THE RICH COTTAGE CHEESE FILLING: Combine the cottage cheese, eggs, mozzarella, Parmesan, basil, and salt in a bowl.

ASSEMBLE: Spread 1 cup of the meat sauce in the bottom of the prepared dish. Top with one-third of the cabbage leaves, one-third of the cottage cheese filling, and one-third of the sauce. Repeat twice in this order: one-third of the cabbage leaves, one-third of the cottage cheese mixture, and one-third of the sauce. Sprinkle the top evenly with the mozzarella and Parmesan.

BAKE, UNCOVERED, for 30 minutes until golden brown and bubbly. Let stand for 15 minutes before serving.

Beef Enchilada Lasagna

I created this simple enchilada sauce years ago and prefer the flavor over canned grocery-store versions. It's simple, and all the ingredients can be kept in the pantry for last-minute cravings. If you need a shortcut, you can buy two (ten-ounce) cans or use two cups of prepared salsa.

~~~~ **SERVES 8** ~~~~

ENCHILADA SAUCE

- 2 cups beef, chicken, or vegetable broth
- 2 tablespoons all-purpose flour
- 1 tablespoon chili powder
- 2 tablespoons tomato paste
- 2 tablespoons apple cider vinegar
- 1 tablespoon ground cumin
- 2 teaspoons minced chipotle peppers in adobo sauce
- ½ teaspoon garlic powder
- ½ teaspoon fine sea salt

GREEN CHILE MEAT SAUCE

- 1 tablespoon extra-virgin olive oil
- 1 onion, chopped
- 1½ pounds lean ground beef
- 2 garlic cloves, minced
- 2 teaspoons ground cumin
- ½ teaspoon fine sea salt
- 1 roasted poblano pepper, seeded and diced, or 1 (7-ounce) can chopped green chilies

COTTAGE CHEESE FILLING

- 1 (16-ounce) container cottage cheese
- 1 large egg
- ¼ teaspoon fine sea salt

- 12 (4-inch) corn tortillas
- 2 cups (8 ounces) shredded cheddar or Mexican-flavored cheese blend
- 1 large tomato, seeded and chopped
- 4 sliced green onions

PREHEAT THE OVEN to 350°F. Lightly grease a 13 x 9-inch baking dish.

MAKE THE ENCHILADA SAUCE: Combine the broth, flour, chili powder, tomato paste, vinegar, cumin, chipotle peppers, garlic powder, and salt in a small saucepan over medium heat. Cook, stirring occasionally, for 5 minutes or until the mixture thickens.

MAKE THE GREEN CHILE MEAT SAUCE: Heat the oil in a large skillet over medium-high. Add the onion and beef. Cook, stirring occasionally, for 10 minutes or until the meat is brown and crumbly. Stir in the garlic, cumin, and salt. Cook, stirring occasionally, for 2 to 3 minutes. Stir in the poblano and 1 cup of the Enchilada Sauce.

MAKE THE COTTAGE CHEESE FILLING: Combine the cottage cheese, egg, and salt in a small bowl.

ASSEMBLE: Spread half the meat sauce in the bottom of the prepared dish. Top with 6 tortillas, overlapping the edges. Layer in this order: the cottage cheese filling, the remaining half of the meat mixture, 1 cup cheddar cheese, remaining 6 tortillas, then remaining cup cheddar cheese. Drizzle the remaining 1 cup of Enchilada Sauce over the top.

COVER AND BAKE for 25 minutes. Uncover and bake for 10 minutes more or until golden brown and bubbly. Let stand for 10 minutes before serving. Sprinkle with the tomato and green onions.

34

Greek Pastitsio Lasagna

A mix of ground beef and ground lamb is traditional in this flavorful and unique Greek specialty. Since the meat is highly seasoned, you won't miss the blend, so go ahead and take a shortcut by using just one type of ground meat. You can even substitute ground turkey or use vegetarian meat crumbles. Be sure to gradually add the hot béchamel mixture to the eggs and yogurt so the eggs do not cook and curdle.

~~~~~~~~~~ **SERVES 8** ~~~~~~~~~~

10 lasagna noodles

SPICED MEAT SAUCE

1 tablespoon extra-virgin olive oil

1 onion, chopped

1 pound ground lean beef or lamb

2 garlic cloves, minced

⅓ cup dry red wine

2 teaspoons ground cinnamon

1 teaspoon fine sea salt

½ teaspoon freshly ground black pepper

½ teaspoon dried oregano

½ teaspoon dried thyme

3 cups seasoned tomato sauce

YOGURT BÉCHAMEL SAUCE

4 tablespoons butter

¼ cup all-purpose flour

2 cups half and half or whole milk

¼ teaspoon ground nutmeg

½ teaspoon fine sea salt

¼ teaspoon freshly ground black pepper

¾ cup (3 ounces) shredded Parmesan cheese

2 large eggs

1 (7-ounce) container (¾ cup) plain Greek yogurt

¾ cup (3 ounces) shredded or grated Parmesan cheese

PREHEAT THE OVEN to 350°F. Lightly grease a 13 x 9-inch baking dish.

COOK THE LASAGNA NOODLES in boiling salted water according to the package directions. Drain, then rinse with cool water.

MAKE THE SPICED MEAT SAUCE: Heat the oil in a large skillet over medium-high. Add the onion and cook, stirring frequently, for 5 minutes until tender. Add the beef and garlic. Cook, stirring frequently, until the meat is crumbled and browned. (Drain the excess oil, if necessary.) Stir in the wine and cook, stirring occasionally, about 2 minutes or until the liquid evaporates. Stir in the cinnamon, salt, pepper, oregano, and thyme. Add the tomato sauce, stirring until well blended. Cook, stirring occasionally, over medium-low heat for 20 minutes.

MAKE THE YOGURT BÉCHAMEL SAUCE: Melt the butter in a large skillet over medium-high heat. Whisk in the flour and cook, stirring constantly, for 1 minute. Whisk in the half and half, nutmeg, salt, and pepper. Cook, stirring frequently, for 5 minutes until the mixture thickens. Stir in the Parmesan cheese. Whisk together the eggs and yogurt in a small bowl. Gradually stir the warm mixture into the yogurt mixture.

ASSEMBLE: Spread ½ cup of the béchamel sauce in the bottom of the prepared dish. Top with 5 noodles. Top with half the meat sauce, 5 more noodles, and the remaining half of the meat sauce. Pour the remaining béchamel sauce evenly over the top. Sprinkle with the Parmesan cheese.

BAKE, UNCOVERED, for 1 hour. Let stand for 10 minutes before slicing.

MEAT

Meaty Mushroom & Alfredo Lasagna

I find a 9 x 9-inch baking dish or pan just the right size to make a hearty, thick serving. An 8 x 8-inch dish is a bit too small, so if you don't have a 9 x 9, use a 13 x 9-inch pan. You may not find the exact ounce measurement for the packages of mushrooms since brands vary. Go ahead and substitute two (eight-ounce) packages of regular button mushrooms and use the 13 x 9-inch pan.

~~~~~~~~ **SERVES 4 TO 6** ~~~~~~~~

8 lasagna noodles

MUSHROOM MEAT SAUCE

1 tablespoon extra-virgin olive oil

1 onion, chopped

1 pound ground beef

3 garlic cloves, chopped

1 tablespoon chopped fresh rosemary

1 teaspoon fine sea salt

½ teaspoon freshly ground black pepper

2 (5-ounce) packages sliced shiitake mushrooms

¾ cup red wine

1 (16-ounce) container refrigerated Alfredo sauce (about 2 cups)

2 cups (8 ounces) shredded mozzarella and/or provolone cheese

PREHEAT THE OVEN to 350°F. Lightly grease a 9 x 9-inch baking dish.

COOK THE LASAGNA NOODLES in boiling salted water according to the package directions. Drain, then rinse in cool water.

MAKE THE MUSHROOM MEAT SAUCE: Heat the olive oil in a large skillet over medium-high. Add the onion and cook, stirring occasionally, for 5 minutes until tender. Add the beef, garlic, rosemary, salt, and pepper. Cook, stirring occasionally, for 10 minutes until the beef is browned and crumbly. Add the mushrooms and wine. Cook, stirring frequently, for 10 minutes until the mushrooms are cooked and the liquid reduces.

ASSEMBLE: Spread ¼ cup of the meat sauce in the bottom of the prepared dish. Top with 4 noodles, cutting and overlapping pieces to fit. Top with half the meat sauce, half the Alfredo sauce, and half the cheese. Repeat with the remaining 4 noodles, meat sauce, Alfredo sauce, and cheese.

BAKE, UNCOVERED, for 30 minutes until golden brown and bubbly. Let stand for 10 minutes before serving.

MEAT

37

Cast-Iron Skillet
Beef & Sausage Lasagna

You can keep the pots and pans to a minimum with this rich
and tasty lasagna that's cooked and baked in the same skillet.
Cast-iron is ideal—it heats evenly and cools slowly so your
dinner stays warm for a round of second servings.

~~~ **SERVES 6** ~~~

RICOTTA FILLING

1 (15-ounce) container ricotta cheese

¼ cup (1 ounce) shredded Parmesan cheese

1 large egg

½ teaspoon fine sea salt

2 tablespoons chopped fresh Italian parsley

MEAT SAUCE

2 teaspoons extra-virgin olive oil

¼ pound spicy Italian sausage, casings removed

¼ pound lean ground beef

¼ onion, chopped

2 garlic cloves, chopped

½ teaspoon Italian seasoning

2 cups pasta or marinara sauce

6 oven-ready lasagna noodles

1 cup (4 ounces) shredded mozzarella cheese

¼ cup (1 ounce) shredded Parmesan cheese

Chopped fresh Italian parsley

PREHEAT THE OVEN to 375°F.

MAKE THE RICOTTA FILLING:
Combine the ricotta, Parmesan, egg, salt, and parsley in a medium bowl.

MAKE THE MEAT SAUCE:
Heat the oil in a 10-inch cast-iron skillet over medium-high. Add the sausage, beef, onion, garlic, and Italian seasoning. Cook, stirring frequently, for 8 to 10 minutes or until the meat is brown and crumbly. Stir in the pasta sauce. Transfer to a bowl (there's no need to clean the skillet).

ASSEMBLE: Spoon ½ cup of the meat sauce into the bottom of the skillet. Top with 3 noodles, breaking them as necessary to make a complete layer. Top with half of the remaining sauce and half the ricotta mixture. Repeat with the remaining 3 noodles, sauce, and ricotta mixture. Sprinkle the top with the mozzarella and Parmesan cheeses.

BAKE, UNCOVERED,
for 40 minutes until hot and bubbly. Broil, if desired, for 2 minutes or until golden brown and bubbly. Let stand for 10 minutes before serving. Sprinkle with the parsley.

Sweet & Spicy Sausage Lasagna

A mix of sweet and spicy Italian sausage gives this basic lasagna just the right amount of heat. You can substitute vegetarian or "meatless" sausage, but you will need to add about one tablespoon of olive oil in the skillet since the veggie types will stick.

〜〜〜〜〜〜〜〜〜 **SERVES 8** 〜〜〜〜〜〜〜〜〜

SWEET & SPICY MEAT SAUCE

- ½ **pound sweet Italian link sausage, casings removed**
- ½ **pound spicy Italian link sausage, casings removed**
- 1 **onion, chopped**
- 2 **garlic cloves, chopped**
- 1 **teaspoon Italian seasoning**
- 1 **(24-ounce) jar pasta or marinara sauce**

RICOTTA-BASIL FILLING

- 1 **(15-ounce) container ricotta cheese**
- 1 **cup (4 ounces) shredded mozzarella cheese**
- ¼ **cup (1 ounce) shredded or grated Parmesan cheese**
- 2 **tablespoons chopped fresh basil**
- 1 **large egg**
- ½ **teaspoon fine sea salt**
- ½ **teaspoon freshly ground black pepper**

- 9 **oven-ready lasagna noodles**
- ½ **cup (2 ounces) shredded mozzarella cheese**
- ¾ **cup (3 ounces) shredded or grated Parmesan cheese**

PREHEAT THE OVEN to 375°F. Lightly grease a 13 x 9-inch baking dish.

MAKE THE SWEET AND SPICY MEAT SAUCE: Combine the sausage, onion, garlic, and Italian seasoning in a large skillet over medium heat. Cook, stirring frequently, for 10 minutes until the sausage is crumbled and cooked through and the onion is tender. Stir in the pasta sauce and set aside.

MAKE THE RICOTTA-BASIL FILLING: Combine the ricotta, mozzarella, Parmesan, basil, egg, salt, and pepper in a bowl, stirring until well blended.

ASSEMBLE: Spoon 1½ cups of the meat sauce into the bottom of the baking dish. Place 3 noodles on top of the sauce. Spread 1 cup of the cheese mixture over the noodles. Repeat two more times in this order: 1 cup of the meat sauce, 3 noodles, and 1 cup of the cheese mixture. Finish with the remaining meat sauce. Sprinkle the top with the mozzarella and Parmesan cheeses.

COVER THE LASAGNA with aluminum foil and bake for 30 minutes. Uncover and bake an additional 20 to 30 minutes until the lasagna is hot and bubbly and the top is golden brown. Let stand for 10 minutes before serving.

Slow Cooker
Sausage & Zucchini Lasagna

I use this easy recipe when I want the homemade taste of lasagna but don't have the time to boil noodles or cook a complicated sauce. The key is using a well-seasoned sausage and pasta sauce. If you have mild or plain versions, stir in a teaspoon of Italian seasoning and about one-eighth or more teaspoon of crushed red pepper flakes. Vegetarians can use the meatless crumbles, and the smoky, chipotle-flavored versions add a lot of flavor.

~~~~~~~~~~~~~~~~ **SERVES 8** ~~~~~~~~~~~~~~~~

- 1 pound ground spicy Italian sausage
- 2 zucchini, chopped
- 4 cups pasta or marinara sauce
- 9 lasagna noodles
- 1 (15-ounce) container ricotta cheese
- 2 cups (8 ounces) shredded mozzarella cheese
- ½ cup (2 ounces) shredded Parmesan or Romano cheese

COMBINE THE SAUSAGE AND ZUCCHINI in a large skillet over medium-high heat. Cook, stirring frequently, until the sausage is browned and crumbly and the zucchini is tender.

ASSEMBLE: Lightly grease the inside of a 6-quart slow cooker. Pour 1 cup of the pasta sauce in the bottom. Top the sauce with 3 noodles, breaking them to fit in an even layer. Dollop half of the ricotta over the noodles. Top with half of the sausage mixture and ½ cup of the mozzarella cheese. Top with 1 cup of the sauce.

REPEAT LAYERING IN THIS ORDER: 3 noodles, remaining ricotta, remaining sausage mixture, ½ cup mozzarella, 1 cup sauce, remaining 3 noodles, remaining cup sauce, remaining cup mozzarella, and the Parmesan.

COVER WITH THE SLOW COOKER LID. Cook on high for 3 to 4 hours or low for 6 to 8 hours. Insert a knife into the lasagna to make sure the noodles are soft. Let stand for 10 minutes before serving.

MEAT

Instant Pot Meat Lasagna

You can shave thirty minutes off the cooking time of a lasagna, dirty fewer pans, and keep your kitchen cooler by using a pressure cooker. Placing a piece of foil over the top before processing keeps the condensation from dripping on the cheese. If you prefer a golden brown top, place the lasagna under a broiler for three or four minutes before removing the sides of the springform pan. Look for a springform pan near multicooker accessories or buy it online. The diameter of the pan will vary depending on the brand, so double-check that the pan will fit easily inside your cooker.

〜〜〜〜〜〜〜〜〜〜 **SERVES 4 TO 6** 〜〜〜〜〜〜〜〜〜〜

BEEF SAUCE

- 1 teaspoon extra-virgin olive oil
- ¼ pound lean ground beef
- 1 (4-ounce) link Italian sausage, casing removed
- ½ small onion, chopped
- 1 garlic clove, minced
- 2 teaspoons Italian seasoning
- 1 tablespoon red wine (optional)
- 2 cups pasta or marinara sauce

RICOTTA FILLING

- 1 cup ricotta cheese
- 1 large egg
- ⅓ cup (1½ ounces) shredded Parmesan cheese

- 6 oven-ready lasagna noodles
- 1 cup (4 ounces) shredded mozzarella cheese

LIGHTLY GREASE a 6½- x 3-inch springform or 3-inch-deep cake pan. Set aside.

MAKE THE BEEF SAUCE: Press Sauté on your multicooker, add the oil, and heat for about 15 seconds. Add the beef, sausage, and onion. Cook, stirring constantly, for 3 to 5 minutes until the meat is cooked and crumbled. Stir in the garlic and Italian seasoning. Cook, stirring frequently, for 2 minutes. Add the wine, if desired, and cook for 1 minute until the liquid evaporates. Transfer the meat mixture to a bowl and stir in the pasta sauce.

MAKE THE RICOTTA FILLING: Combine the ricotta, egg, and Parmesan cheese in a medium bowl.

ASSEMBLE: Spoon ½ cup of the meat sauce into the bottom of the prepared pan. Top with a layer of 2 noodles, breaking pieces to fit. Spread one-third of the ricotta filling on the noodles and top with one-third of the sauce. Repeat twice more in this order: noodles, ricotta, and sauce. Sprinkle the top with the mozzarella cheese.

PLACE A WIRE TRIVET in the bottom of the inner pan of the multicooker. (You can wipe away the oil from the sautéed meat, if desired, but it won't matter if you want to skip.) Pour 1½ cups water in the bottom. If using a foil sling, place it under the lasagna and lower it into the pot. Place a piece of foil over the top of lasagna.

PLACE THE LID ON THE COOKER and turn the vent knob to Seal. Set the cooker to high pressure for 20 minutes. Let stand for 10 minutes for a slow release, then turn the knob to finish releasing any pressure. Carefully lift out the lasagna and place on a plate before releasing the sides of the pan. If desired, place the lasagna on a foil-lined baking sheet and broil for 3 minutes or until browned and bubbly. Let stand for 10 minutes before serving.

Swiss Chard & Sausage Lasagna

This stunning entrée looks complicated, but it's easy to assemble the layers. Bright red- or yellow-stemmed chard looks beautiful, but any color works, as well as substitutes like kale or collard leaves.

~~~~~~~~~ **SERVES 8** ~~~~~~~~~

2 (6-ounce) bunches red, multicolored, or green Swiss chard

SAUSAGE MEAT SAUCE

1 tablespoon extra-virgin olive oil

1 onion, chopped

1 pound ground sage-flavored or spicy Italian sausage

3 garlic cloves, minced

¼ cup dry red wine

½ teaspoon fine sea salt

½ teaspoon freshly ground black pepper

1 teaspoon Italian seasoning

2 cups no-sugar-added pasta or marinara sauce

½ cup sliced ripe olives

RICOTTA FILLING

1 (15-ounce) container ricotta cheese

2 large eggs

¾ cup (3 ounces) shredded Parmesan cheese

¼ teaspoon fine sea salt

¼ teaspoon freshly ground black pepper

PREHEAT THE OVEN to 350°F. Line a 9-inch-round springform or deep-dish cake pan with nonstick foil.

TRIM AWAY THE TOUGH STEMS from the chard, keeping the leaves whole. Slice the stems and set aside. Cook the chard in boiling salted water for 3 minutes until wilted. Drain in a colander, then place on paper towels to dry.

MAKE THE SAUSAGE MEAT SAUCE: Heat the oil in a large skillet over medium-high. Add the onion and reserved chard stems. Cook, stirring frequently, for 3 minutes until tender. Add the sausage and garlic and cook, stirring frequently, until the meat is crumbled and browned. (Drain the excess oil, if necessary.) Stir in the wine and cook, stirring occasionally, until the liquid evaporates. Stir in the salt, pepper, and Italian seasoning. Add the pasta sauce and olives, stirring until well blended. Cook, stirring occasionally, over medium-low heat for 15 to 20 minutes.

MAKE THE RICOTTA FILLING: Combine the ricotta, eggs, Parmesan, salt, and pepper in a medium bowl.

ASSEMBLE: Divide the chard leaves into three portions. Layer one-third of the chard leaves in the bottom of the prepared pan and top with half of the sauce and half of the ricotta filling. Repeat with one-third of the chard, remaining half of the sauce, and remaining half of the ricotta. Arrange the remaining chard on top.

BAKE, UNCOVERED, for 40 minutes. Let stand for 15 minutes before serving. Invert the lasagna on a serving platter.

MEAT

Braised Short Rib & Mushroom Lasagna

The rich and savory aroma of the braised short ribs will fill your kitchen with a mouthwatering scent. No one will shame you if you occasionally skip the lasagna process and just make the short ribs, served over mashed potatoes or polenta! Short ribs have a lot of fat on them (but that's key to their amazing flavor), and you'll have a few opportunities to skim off any excess oil before assembling.

SERVES 8

SHORT RIB FILLING

2½ to 3 pounds beef short ribs

½ teaspoon fine sea salt

½ teaspoon freshly ground black pepper

2 tablespoons extra-virgin olive oil

2 celery stalks, chopped

1 large carrot, peeled and chopped

2 garlic cloves, chopped

10 to 12 ounces mixed wild mushrooms, sliced

2 cups beef broth

1 cup red wine

2 tablespoons tomato paste

1 bay leaf

BASIC BÉCHAMEL SAUCE

2 tablespoons salted butter

3 tablespoons all-purpose flour

2½ cups whole milk

¼ teaspoon fine sea salt

¼ teaspoon ground nutmeg

6 lasagna noodles

¾ cup (3 ounces) shredded Parmesan cheese

PREHEAT THE OVEN to 375°F. Lightly grease a 9 x 9-inch baking dish.

MAKE THE SHORT RIB FILLING: Sprinkle the short ribs with the salt and pepper. Heat the oil in a Dutch oven or heavy, deep skillet over medium-high heat. Add the short ribs and cook for 3 minutes on each side until browned. Transfer to a plate. Drain the excess oil from the pan, leaving 1 tablespoon to coat the bottom. Heat this remaining oil over medium. Add the celery, carrots, garlic, and mushrooms. Cook, stirring frequently, for 5 minutes. Combine the broth, wine, tomato paste, and bay leaf in a small bowl, then stir into the mushroom mixture. Add the reserved beef. Cover and bake for 2½ to 3 hours until the meat is very tender and pulls easily off the bone. Remove and discard the bay leaf. Transfer the beef ribs to a cutting board and let stand until cool enough to handle. While the beef cools, skim off any excess fat from the top of the mushroom mixture. Remove the bones and tough inedible pieces of meat and discard. Shred the meat into bite-size pieces and stir back into the mushroom mixture.

MAKE THE BASIC BÉCHAMEL SAUCE: Melt the butter in a large skillet over medium-high heat. Whisk in the flour and cook, stirring constantly, for 1 minute. Whisk in the milk, salt, and nutmeg. Cook, stirring frequently, for 5 minutes until the mixture thickens.

COOK THE NOODLES in boiling salted water to cover according to the package directions. Drain, then rinse with cool water.

ASSEMBLE: Spoon ½ cup of the béchamel sauce on the bottom of the prepared dish and top with 3 noodles, cutting to fit the pan. Add half of the meat mixture and half of the sauce. Repeat with the remaining noodles, beef, and sauce. Sprinkle with the Parmesan cheese.

COVER AND BAKE for 30 minutes. Uncover and bake for 15 minutes until golden brown and bubbly. Let stand for 10 minutes before serving.

Asian Short Rib Lasagna

If there was one word I would use to describe this dish, it's umami—the fifth category of taste that corresponds to savory and often comes from foods like beef and soy sauce. If I don't want to heat up the kitchen or babysit food on the stovetop, I cook the short ribs in a slow cooker. Brown them as directed, then transfer the ribs and the liquid to a slow cooker and cook on high for four hours or low for eight hours.

SERVES 4 TO 6

SHORT RIB FILLING

- 1 tablespoon extra-virgin olive oil
- 2½ pounds beef short ribs
- 1 cup beef broth
- ⅔ cup low-sodium soy sauce
- ¼ cup dark brown sugar
- 2 tablespoons minced fresh ginger
- 2 garlic cloves, sliced
- 2 (3-inch) pieces fresh lemongrass, halved (optional)
- 2 tablespoons toasted sesame oil
- 2 tablespoons sriracha sauce
- 2 tablespoon rice vinegar

SWISS WHITE SAUCE

- 3 tablespoons reserved oil from short ribs, or butter
- 3 tablespoons all-purpose flour
- 2 cups whole milk
- 1 cup (4 ounces) shredded Swiss cheese

- 3 cups torn Napa cabbage leaves or chopped baby bok choy
- 18 refrigerated wonton wrappers or 6 egg roll wrappers
- ½ cup (2 ounces) shredded or grated Parmesan cheese
- 3 chopped green onions

PREHEAT THE OVEN to 350°F. Lightly grease an 8 x 8-inch or 9 x 9-inch baking dish.

MAKE THE SHORT RIB FILLING: Heat the oil in a Dutch oven or deep, heavy skillet over medium-high. Add the short ribs and cook for 3 minutes on each side until browned. Transfer to a plate and drain away the oil. Combine the broth, soy sauce, brown sugar, ginger, garlic, lemongrass (if using), sesame oil, sriracha, and vinegar in the Dutch oven, stirring until well blended. Return the beef ribs to the liquid, bone side up. Cover and bake for 2½ to 3 hours or until the meat is very tender. Transfer the beef ribs to a cutting board and let stand until cool enough to handle. Skim off 3 tablespoons oil from the top of the cooking liquid for the next step and set aside an additional ¼ cup cooking liquid. Remove the bones and tough inedible pieces of meat and discard. Shred the meat into bite-size pieces. Transfer to a bowl and drizzle with the reserved ¼ cup liquid.

MAKE THE SWISS WHITE SAUCE: Heat the reserved oil from the short rib braising liquid in a large skillet over medium-high. Whisk in the flour and cook, stirring constantly, for 1 minute. Whisk in the milk and cook, stirring frequently, for 5 minutes until the mixture thickens. Add the Swiss cheese and stir until the cheese melts and the mixture is smooth.

BLANCH THE CABBAGE in boiling water for 5 minutes until wilted. Drain on a wire rack and pat dry with paper towels.

ASSEMBLE: Spread ½ cup of the Swiss White Sauce in the bottom of the prepared baking dish. Top with 6 wonton wrappers. Top with one-third of the beef mixture, one-third of the cabbage, and one-third of the white sauce. Repeat twice in this order: 6 wonton wrappers, one-third of the beef mixture, one-third of the cabbage, and one-third of the sauce. Sprinkle with the Parmesan cheese.

BAKE for 35 to 40 minutes until golden brown and bubbly. Let stand for 10 minutes before serving. Sprinkle with the green onions.

Barbecue Brisket Lasagna

Smoky barbecue meat is a great base for a rich and satisfying lasagna. I find using only barbecue sauce a bit intense, so I mix it with a plain pasta sauce.

10 lasagna noodles

1 cup prepared barbecue sauce

1 cup pasta or marinara sauce

1½ pounds (about 6 cups) chopped smoked brisket, pulled pork, or chicken

RICOTTA FILLING

1 (15-ounce) container ricotta or cottage cheese

1 large egg

¼ teaspoon fine sea salt

¼ teaspoon freshly ground black pepper

¼ cup chopped fresh parsley

3 cups (12 ounces) shredded cheddar, smoked provolone, or Swiss cheese

PREHEAT THE OVEN to 350°F. Lightly grease a 13 x 9-inch baking dish.

COOK THE LASAGNA NOODLES in boiling salted water according to the package directions. Drain, then rinse in cool water.

STIR TOGETHER the barbecue and pasta sauces in a large bowl. Set aside ¼ cup. Add the brisket to the large bowl and toss to coat.

MAKE THE RICOTTA FILLING: Combine the ricotta, egg, salt, pepper, and parsley in a bowl.

ASSEMBLE: Spread the reserved ¼ cup sauce in the bottom of the prepared dish. Top with 5 lasagna noodles. Add one half of the ricotta filling, one half of the meat, and 1 cup of the cheddar cheese. Repeat with the remaining 5 noodles, ricotta filling, and meat. Top evenly with the remaining 2 cups of cheddar cheese.

COVER AND BAKE for 30 minutes. Uncover and broil for 3 to 5 minutes, until the top is golden brown and bubbly. Let stand for 10 minutes before serving.

Philly Cheesesteak Lasagna

Well-marbled and tender beef rib eye is a delicious choice, but you can use any cut here you prefer. Round or flank steak can be tough, so make sure you cut the slices very thin. You can even use a lean ground beef or turkey, which can be sautéed with the peppers and onion.

〜〜〜〜〜〜〜〜〜〜〜 **SERVES 4** 〜〜〜〜〜〜〜〜〜〜〜

12 lasagna noodles

PHILLY CHEESESTEAK FILLING

1 tablespoon extra-virgin olive oil

1 (12- to 16-ounce) beef rib eye or other boneless steak, cut into thin strips

1 red bell pepper, sliced

1 green bell pepper, sliced

1 onion, halved and sliced

¼ teaspoon fine sea salt

¼ teaspoon freshly ground pepper

PROVOLONE CHEESE SAUCE

3 tablespoons butter

3 tablespoons all-purpose flour

2½ cups whole milk

2 cups (8 ounces) shredded provolone cheese

1 teaspoon Italian seasoning

½ teaspoon fine sea salt

½ teaspoon freshly ground black pepper

1 cup (4 ounces) shredded mozzarella

PREHEAT THE OVEN to 350°F. Lightly grease a 9 x 9-inch baking dish.

COOK THE LASAGNA NOODLES in boiling salted water according to the package directions. Drain, then rinse in cool water.

MAKE THE PHILLY CHEESESTEAK FILLING: Heat the oil in a large skillet over medium-high. Add the steak strips and cook, stirring frequently, for 5 minutes until done. Transfer to a large bowl. Add the bell peppers and onion to the skillet and cook, stirring frequently, for 5 to 7 minutes until tender. Transfer to the bowl. Stir in the salt and pepper.

MAKE THE PROVOLONE CHEESE SAUCE: Melt the butter in a large skillet over medium heat. Add the flour and cook, stirring constantly, for 1 minute. Whisk in the milk and cook, stirring frequently, for 5 minutes until thickened. Add the provolone, Italian seasoning, salt, and pepper. Cook, stirring frequently, until smooth.

ASSEMBLE: Spread ¾ cup of the cheese sauce in the bottom of the prepared dish. Top with 4 noodles, cutting to fit in the pan. Top the noodles with one-third of the Philly Cheesesteak Filling and one-third of the cheese sauce. Repeat twice in this order: noodles, Philly Cheesesteak Filling, and cheese sauce. Sprinkle the lasagna with the mozzarella.

COVER AND BAKE for 30 minutes. Uncover and bake for 15 minutes until golden brown and bubbly. Let stand for 10 minutes before serving.

MEAT

Hash Brown Breakfast Lasagna

Layer healthy vegetables with seasoned hash browns
for a hearty breakfast that feeds a crowd!

~~~~~~~~~~~~~~~~~~~~~~~~ **SERVES 10 TO 12** ~~~~~~~~~~~~~~~~~~~~~~~~

HAM & VEGGIE FILLING

1 tablespoon extra-virgin olive oil

1 onion, chopped

1 green bell pepper, chopped

1 red or yellow bell pepper, chopped

1 (8-ounce) package mushrooms, sliced

½ teaspoon fine sea salt

¼ teaspoon freshly ground black pepper

2½ cups (12 ounces) chopped cooked ham

SCRAMBLED EGGS

1 dozen large eggs

2½ cups whole milk

½ teaspoon fine sea salt

¼ teaspoon freshly ground black pepper

2 (20-ounce) bags refrigerated seasoned hash browns

2 cups (8-ounces) shredded cheddar cheese

PREHEAT OVEN to 375°F. Lightly grease a 13 x 9-inch baking dish.

MAKE THE HAM & VEGGIE FILLING: Heat the oil in a large skillet over medium-high. Add the onion, bell peppers, mushrooms, salt, and pepper. Cook, stirring frequently, for 7 to 10 minutes until vegetables are tender. Drain any excess liquid, if necessary. Stir in the ham.

MAKE THE SCRAMBLED EGGS: Whisk together the eggs, milk, salt, and pepper in a large bowl.

ASSEMBLE: Spread half of the hash browns in the bottom of the prepared baking dish. Spread half of the vegetable filling over the hash browns, and half of the cheese. Repeat with the remaining half hash browns, vegetable filling, and cheese.

POUR THE SCRAMBLED EGGS over the top of the lasagna. Cover and let stand for 5 minutes until the egg mixture has soaked through all the layers.

BAKE, UNCOVERED, for 45 to 55 minutes, until the eggs are cooked and the top is golden brown. Let stand for 10 minutes before serving.

Ham & Cheese Lasagna

Honey, mustard, and ham are flavors meant to be paired. Suitable for all ages, this tomato sauce–free lasagna is a favorite among kids.

〜〜〜〜〜〜 **SERVES 8** 〜〜〜〜〜〜

HONEY-DIJON BÉCHAMEL

4 tablespoons butter

1 small onion, chopped

3 tablespoons all-purpose flour

3 cups whole milk

¼ cup Dijon mustard

1 tablespoon honey

1 teaspoon fresh thyme leaves

¼ teaspoon fine sea salt

1 cup (4 ounces) shredded Swiss cheese

12 oven-ready lasagna noodles

2 cups chopped cooked ham

1 cup (4 ounces) shredded Swiss cheese

1 cup packaged fried onions

PREHEAT THE OVEN to 375°F. Lightly grease a 13 x 9-inch baking dish.

MAKE THE HONEY-DIJON BÉCHAMEL: Melt the butter in a large skillet over medium-high heat. Add the onion and cook, stirring frequently, for 5 minutes. Add the flour and cook, stirring constantly, for 1 minute. Whisk in the milk, mustard, honey, thyme, and salt. Cook, stirring frequently, for 5 to 7 minutes or until the sauce thickens. Add the Swiss cheese, stirring until smooth.

ASSEMBLE: Spread ½ cup of the sauce in the bottom of the prepared dish. Top with 4 noodles, breaking to fit. Top with one-third of the ham and one-third of the remaining sauce. Repeat two more times in this order: 4 noodles, one-third ham, and one-third sauce. Sprinkle the top with the Swiss cheese and fried onions.

COVER AND BAKE for 30 minutes. Uncover and bake for 10 minutes until golden brown and bubbly. Let stand for 10 minutes before serving.

Egg & Bacon
Breakfast Lasagna

Try this twist on basic breakfast flavors when you need something a bit different to serve for company that can also be made the night before. (When you don't want to wake up super early to prep!) Substitute Canadian bacon or vegetarian bacon. I used olive oil to sauté the onion as it's heart healthy, but the bacon drippings would provide a fuller flavor.

SERVES 10

12 ounces bacon, chopped

CHEDDAR SAUCE
3 tablespoons extra-virgin olive oil

1 small sweet onion, chopped

4 tablespoons all-purpose flour

3 cups whole milk

½ teaspoon freshly ground black pepper

1 cup (4 ounces) shredded cheddar cheese

8 to 10 oven-ready lasagna noodles

1 dozen hard-boiled large eggs, peeled and sliced

1 cup (4 ounces) shredded cheddar cheese

1 tablespoon chopped fresh Italian parsley

LIGHTLY GREASE a 13 x 9-inch baking dish.

COOK THE BACON in a large skillet over medium heat until crispy. Remove with a slotted spoon and drain on paper towels.

MAKE THE CHEDDAR SAUCE: Heat the oil in the skillet over medium heat. Add the onion and cook, stirring frequently, for 5 minutes until tender. Stir in the flour and cook, stirring constantly, for 1 minute. Whisk in the milk and pepper and cook, stirring frequently, for 5 minutes until slightly thickened. Stir in 1 cup of the cheese. Cook, stirring frequently, until smooth.

ASSEMBLE: Spread ½ cup of the cheese sauce in the bottom of the prepared dish. Top with 4 to 5 noodles. Spread one-third of the sauce over the noodles. Arrange half of the eggs on top and sprinkle with half of the bacon. Repeat layers in this order: 4 to 5 noodles, sauce, eggs, bacon, and remaining sauce. Sprinkle with the cheddar cheese. Cover and refrigerate up to a day ahead.

PREHEAT THE OVEN to 350°F. Bake, covered, for 30 minutes. Uncover and bake for 10 minutes until golden brown. Let stand for 10 minutes before serving. Sprinkle with the parsley.

MEAT

Noodle-Free Sweet Potato & Chorizo Lasagna

Planks of cooked sweet potato substitute for traditional noodles to make this yummy concoction gluten-free and keto-friendly.

SERVES 4

2 large sweet potatoes

CILANTRO PESTO

1 cup fresh cilantro leaves and stems

2 tablespoons extra-virgin olive oil

1 teaspoon lime zest

1 tablespoon fresh lime juice

1 garlic clove, chopped

½ teaspoon ground cumin

¼ teaspoon fine sea salt

RICOTTA FILLING

1 (15-ounce) container ricotta cheese

1 large egg

½ cup (2 ounces) shredded Parmesan cheese

¼ teaspoon fine sea salt

CHORIZO SAUCE

1 tablespoon extra-virgin olive oil

½ onion, chopped

10 to 12 ounces Mexican chorizo or soy-based chorizo sausage

1 (14.5-ounce) can diced fire-roasted tomatoes, undrained

1 cup (4 ounces) shredded Monterey Jack or queso fresco cheese

Chopped fresh cilantro

PREHEAT THE OVEN to 350°F. Lightly grease an 8-cup or 8 x 8-inch baking dish.

WRAP THE SWEET POTATOES in aluminum foil and bake directly on the oven rack for 30 to 40 minutes until tender. Cool completely, peel, and slice. If desired, you can also microwave the potatoes, unwrapped, on high for 5 minutes until tender. (They may be prepared up to 3 days in advance.)

MAKE THE CILANTRO PESTO: Combine the cilantro, olive oil, lime zest and juice, garlic, cumin, and salt in a blender or small food processor. Process until finely chopped. Cover and refrigerate, up to 1 day in advance, until ready to assemble. If desired, you can finely chop all of these ingredients and stir together.

MAKE THE RICOTTA FILLING: Combine the ricotta, egg, Parmesan, and salt in a bowl.

MAKE THE CHORIZO SAUCE: Heat the oil in a large skillet over medium-high. Add the onion and cook, stirring frequently, for 3 to 5 minutes until tender. Add the chorizo and cook, stirring frequently, until crumbled and browned. Spoon away any excess oil. Stir in the diced tomatoes and cook, stirring occasionally, until the mixture is hot and slightly thickened.

ASSEMBLE: Pour half of the chorizo sauce into the bottom of the prepared dish. Top with half of the sweet potato slices, half of the ricotta cheese mixture, and drizzle with half of the cilantro pesto. Repeat with remaining sweet potatoes, sauce, ricotta mixture, and pesto. Sprinkle with the Monterey Jack cheese.

COVER AND BAKE for 30 minutes. Uncover and bake for 10 minutes until golden brown. Let stand for 10 minutes before serving. Sprinkle with cilantro.

MEAT

Pesto, Peppers & Prosciutto Lasagna

A bit of fresh lemon keeps the bright green color in pesto. For a twist, substitute arugula for the basil and walnuts or almonds for the pine nuts. Toasting the nuts enhances the texture and flavor. I will toast large quantities in the oven, then freeze them until I need to add a bit of crunch to salads, sandwiches, or cheese appetizers.

~~~~~~~~~~~~~~~~~~ **SERVES 8** ~~~~~~~~~~~~~~~~~~

PESTO SAUCE

2 cups lightly packed fresh basil

2 garlic cloves

⅔ cup (2½ ounces) shredded or grated Parmesan cheese

½ cup extra-virgin olive oil

½ teaspoon lemon zest

1 tablespoon lemon juice

½ teaspoon fine sea salt

3 tablespoons toasted pine nuts

BASIC BÉCHAMEL SAUCE

2 tablespoons butter

2 tablespoons all-purpose flour

2½ cups whole milk

¼ teaspoon fine sea salt

¼ teaspoon freshly ground black pepper

¼ teaspoon ground nutmeg

8 to 12 oven-ready lasagna noodles

4 roasted red bell peppers, thinly sliced or 1 (16-ounce) jar, drained well and thinly sliced

1 cup (4 ounces) grated or shredded Parmesan cheese

2 ounces thinly sliced prosciutto (about 5 slices)

PREHEAT THE OVEN to 350°F. Lightly grease an 11 x 7-inch baking dish.

MAKE THE PESTO SAUCE: Combine the basil, garlic, Parmesan, olive oil, lemon zest and juice, and salt in a food processor; pulse until finely chopped. Add the pine nuts and pulse until finely chopped. Transfer to a large bowl.

MAKE THE BASIC BÉCHAMEL SAUCE: Melt the butter in a large skillet over medium-high heat. Whisk in the flour and cook, stirring constantly, for 1 minute. Whisk in the milk, salt, pepper, and nutmeg. Cook, stirring frequently, for 5 minutes until thickened.

ASSEMBLE: Spread ½ cup of the béchamel sauce in the bottom of the prepared dish and arrange 2 to 3 noodles on top, breaking to fit the pan. Spread one-fourth of the pesto sauce over the noodles and top with one-fourth of the roasted peppers, one-fourth of the béchamel sauce, and one-fourth of the Parmesan cheese. Repeat three more times in this order: noodles, pesto, peppers, béchamel, and cheese. Arrange the prosciutto over the top.

BAKE, UNCOVERED, for 50 to 60 minutes until the noodles are tender and the top is golden brown. Let stand for 10 minutes before serving.

Pepperoni Lasagna

Although very similar to pasta sauce, pizza sauce is usually uncooked before using and often has a distinct oregano flavor. In a rush, you can substitute three cups of prepared pizza pasta sauce. I like black olives, but you can substitute any topping you prefer. Consider chopped artichoke hearts, sautéed mushrooms, or green bell pepper.

~~~~~~~~~~~ **SERVES 8** ~~~~~~~~~~~

PIZZA SAUCE

1 (28-ounce) can crushed tomatoes

1 (6-ounce) can tomato paste

1 tablespoon Italian seasoning

2 teaspoons dried oregano

1 teaspoon fine sea salt

½ teaspoon garlic powder

⅛ teaspoon crushed red pepper flakes

Pinch sugar

RICOTTA FILLING

1 (15-ounce) container ricotta cheese

1 cup (4 ounces) shredded mozzarella cheese

1 large egg

¼ teaspoon fine sea salt

¼ teaspoon freshly ground pepper

9 to 12 oven-ready lasagna noodles

½ (6-ounce) package sliced pepperoni

¼ cup sliced black olives

1 cup (4 ounces) shredded or grated Parmesan cheese

PREHEAT THE OVEN to 375°F. Lightly grease a 13 x 9-inch baking dish.

MAKE THE PIZZA SAUCE: Combine the tomatoes, tomato paste, Italian seasoning, oregano, salt, garlic powder, red pepper flakes, and sugar in a large bowl.

MAKE THE RICOTTA FILLING: Combine the ricotta, mozzarella, egg, salt, and pepper in a bowl.

ASSEMBLE: Spread ½ cup of the pizza sauce in the bottom of the prepared pan. Top with 3 to 4 noodles, breaking to fit in an even layer. Spread with 1 cup of the pizza sauce and arrange one-third of the pepperoni on top. Dollop with half of the ricotta filling. Repeat again with 3 to 4 noodles, 1 cup pizza sauce, one-third of the pepperoni, and the remaining ricotta filling. Top with 3 to 4 noodles and the remaining sauce. Spread the remaining pepperoni slices and black olives over the top.

COVER AND BAKE for 45 minutes. (Insert a knife in the center to make sure the noodles are tender.) Uncover and sprinkle with the Parmesan cheese. Bake for 15 minutes until the pepperoni are cooked and the cheese is melted. Let stand for 10 minutes before serving.

Homemade Keto Noodle Beef Lasagna

Here's another riff on keto noodles inspired by a recipe given to me by my neighbor Sharon Manion's daughter, Cara. This one is cheese and egg based, and I added a bit of almond flour to the mixture to further simulate a traditional noodle. Save the "noodle" recipe to use as a low-carb sandwich wrap; spread the mixture into four seven- to nine-inch circles and bake as directed.

〜〜〜〜〜〜〜 **SERVES 8 TO 10** 〜〜〜〜〜〜〜

KETO NOODLES

3 cups (12 ounces) shredded mozzarella, at room temperature

1 (8-ounce) package cream cheese, softened

½ cup almond flour

3 large eggs

1 teaspoon Italian seasoning

⅛ teaspoon fine sea salt

SPINACH-OLIVE MEAT SAUCE

1 tablespoon extra-virgin olive oil

1 pound ground beef

1 pound spicy Italian sausage, casings removed

½ (6-ounce) package sliced pepperoni, coarsely chopped

3 garlic cloves, minced

1 (28-ounce) can seasoned crushed tomatoes

1 (6-ounce drained weight) can ripe olives, drained and sliced

2 teaspoons Italian seasoning

1 tablespoon fresh chopped rosemary

1 (12- to 16-ounce) package frozen chopped spinach, thawed and drained well

1 cup (4 ounces) shredded mozzarella cheese

1 cup (4 ounces) shredded or grated Parmesan or Romano cheese

PREHEAT THE OVEN to 350°F. Line two sheet pans with parchment paper or nonstick foil. Lightly grease a 13 x 9-inch baking dish.

MAKE THE KETO NOODLES: Combine the mozzarella, cream cheese, almond flour, eggs, Italian seasoning, and salt in a food processor. Process until the mixture is smooth. Spread in a thin, even, rectangular layer measuring 13 x 9 inches on each of the sheet pans. Bake for 15 to 20 minutes until light golden brown, rotating pans halfway through baking.

MAKE THE SPINACH-OLIVE MEAT SAUCE: Heat the oil in a large, deep skillet over medium-high. Add the ground beef, sausage, pepperoni, and garlic. Cook, stirring frequently, for 10 minutes or until the meat is browned and crumbly. Drain excess oil, if necessary. Stir in the tomatoes, olives, Italian seasoning, and rosemary. Add the spinach. Cook, stirring occasionally, for 15 minutes or until the mixture thickens.

ASSEMBLE: Spread 1 cup of the meat sauce in the bottom of the prepared dish. Top with one of the keto noodles and half of the meat sauce. Repeat with the remaining keto noodle and meat sauce. Sprinkle the top with the mozzarella and Parmesan cheeses.

COVER AND BAKE for 30 minutes. Let stand for 10 minutes before serving.

MEAT

POULTRY

Chicken & Green Chili Lasagna **65**

Chicken Florentine Lasagna **66**

Keto or Gluten-Free Chicken
& Artichoke Lasagna **67**

Romesco Grilled Chicken
& Zucchini Lasagna **68**

Chicken & Asparagus Lasagna **70**

Chicken-Ricotta Roll-Up Lasagna **71**

Chicken Piccata Ricotta Lasagna **73**

Roasted Broccoli & Chicken
Lasagna **74**

Chicken Alfredo & Arugula
Pesto Lasagna **76**

Chicken & Caramelized Onion
Lasagna with Blue Cheese
Béchamel **77**

Roasted Butternut Squash
& Chicken Lasagna **79**

Slow Cooker Parmesan-Garlic
Chicken **80**

Chicken Cordon Bleu
Lasagna Rolls **81**

Roasted Garlic, Chicken
& Sweet Potato Lasagna **83**

Mexican Chicken, Black Bean
& Corn Lasagna **84**

Winter Squash Marinara &
Ricotta Lasagna **86**

Turkey Pot Pie Lasagna **87**

Keto-Friendly Turkey Sausage
& Kale Lasagna **89**

Roasted Fall Veggies & Turkey
Lasagna **90**

Chicken & Green Chili Lasagna

You'll see several options of canned green chilies if shopping at larger or international markets. I prefer to use fire-roasted or spicy versions, but you pick the heat level you prefer. My favorite, though more labor intensive, is to grill some fresh hatch or poblano peppers over a grill until the skins char, then seed and dice. If I'm grilling chicken for this dish, I'll go for fresh fire-roasted green chilies, otherwise using the canned type makes this a pantry-friendly recipe.

~~~~~~~~~~~~~~~~~~~~~~ **SERVES 6** ~~~~~~~~~~~~~~~~~~~~~~

CHICKEN FILLING

3 cups shredded rotisserie or cooked chicken

1 (7-ounce) can diced green chilies, drained

1 (2¼-ounce) can sliced ripe olives, drained

½ cup fresh cilantro, chopped

1 cup (4 ounces) shredded cheddar cheese

1 cup (4 ounces) shredded Monterey or Pepper Jack cheese

MEXICAN WHITE SAUCE

2 tablespoons butter

2 tablespoons all-purpose flour

2 cups whole milk

2 teaspoons ground cumin

2 teaspoons chili powder

½ teaspoon garlic powder

½ teaspoon fine sea salt

½ cup sour cream

5 to 6 (7-inch) flour or corn tortillas

1 cup (4 ounces) shredded cheddar cheese

1 cup (4 ounces) shredded Monterey or Pepper Jack cheese

2 Roma tomatoes, sliced

1 jalapeño, sliced

2 tablespoons fresh cilantro leaves

PREHEAT THE OVEN to 375°F. Lightly grease a 13 x 9-inch baking dish.

MAKE THE CHICKEN FILLING: Combine the chicken, chilies, olives, cilantro, cheddar, and Monterey Jack in a large bowl.

MAKE THE MEXICAN WHITE SAUCE: Melt the butter in a large skillet over medium-high heat. Whisk in the flour and cook, stirring constantly, for 1 minute. Whisk in the milk, cumin, chili powder, garlic powder, and salt. Cook, stirring frequently, for 5 minutes until the mixture thickens. Stir in the sour cream.

ASSEMBLE: Spread ½ cup of the Mexican white sauce on the bottom of the prepared baking dish. Top with 1½ to 2 tortillas, cutting into pieces to complete the layer. Spread 2 cups of the chicken filling over the tortillas and drizzle with ½ cup of the white sauce. Repeat twice in this order: a layer of tortillas, 2 cups chicken filling, and ½ cup white sauce. Sprinkle with the cheddar and Monterey Jack cheeses and arrange the tomatoes and jalapeño across the top.

COVER AND BAKE for 30 minutes. Uncover and bake for 15 minutes until golden brown. Let stand for 15 minutes before slicing. Sprinkle with the cilantro.

POULTRY

Chicken Florentine Lasagna

Change it up by substituting arugula or kale for the baby spinach. If you use frozen spinach, thaw and squeeze it well to remove most of the liquid.

~~~~~~~~~ **SERVES 8** ~~~~~~~~~

FLORENTINE WHITE SAUCE

3 tablespoons butter

¼ teaspoon crushed red pepper flakes

2 shallots, minced

3 tablespoons all-purpose flour

¼ cup white wine

2 cups chicken broth

1 cup heavy cream

4 ounces cream cheese

¼ teaspoon fine sea salt

½ teaspoon freshly ground black pepper

¼ teaspoon ground nutmeg

2 (5-ounce) containers baby spinach leaves

CHICKEN FILLING

4 cups shredded rotisserie or chopped cooked chicken

4 slices bacon, cooked and crumbled

½ cup toasted walnuts, chopped

12 oven-ready lasagna noodles

1 cup (4 ounces) shredded Parmesan cheese

½ cup panko breadcrumbs

PREHEAT THE OVEN to 350°F. Lightly grease a 13 x 9-inch baking dish.

MAKE THE FLORENTINE WHITE SAUCE: Melt the butter in a large skillet over medium heat. Add the red pepper flakes and shallots and cook, stirring frequently, for 3 to 5 minutes until the shallots are tender. Whisk in the flour and cook, stirring constantly, for 1 minute. Stir in the wine and the broth. Cook, stirring frequently, for 5 minutes until thickened. Whisk in the cream, cream cheese, salt, pepper, and nutmeg. Cook, stirring frequently, until smooth. Add the spinach, in batches, and cook, stirring occasionally, until wilted.

MAKE THE CHICKEN FILLING: Combine the chicken, bacon, and nuts in a medium bowl.

ASSEMBLE: Spread 1 cup of the Florentine white sauce on the bottom of the prepared dish. Layer with 3 to 4 noodles, breaking them, if necessary, to fit. Top with 1 cup of the white sauce and sprinkle evenly with 1¼ cups of the chicken filling. Layer two more times in this order: 3 to 4 noodles, 1 cup of white sauce, and 1¼ cups of chicken filling. Spread the remaining white sauce over the chicken and sprinkle evenly with the Parmesan and panko.

COVER AND BAKE for 40 minutes. Uncover and bake for 10 minutes until golden brown and bubbly. Let stand for 10 minutes before serving.

Keto or Gluten-Free
Chicken & Artichoke Lasagna

Fans of hot artichoke dip will recognize the main flavor of this very rich and satisfying dish. If I want to keep this as low-carb as possible, I use a packaged vegetable lasagna noodle made from hearts of palm. It's not always easy to find and is a bit expensive, so you can use thinly sliced zucchini as a substitute. If you simply want a gluten-free option, use readily available gluten-free pasta. Of course, traditional lasagna fans can sub whatever type of oven-ready or traditional boiled noodle they prefer.

SERVES 10

KETO CREAM CHEESE SAUCE

2 cups heavy cream

1½ cups whole milk

½ teaspoon garlic powder

¾ teaspoon fine sea salt

½ teaspoon freshly ground black pepper

¼ teaspoon ground nutmeg

¼ teaspoon cayenne pepper

2 (8-ounce) packages cream cheese, softened and cut into large pieces

¼ cup chopped fresh basil

CHICKEN-ARTICHOKE FILLING

3 cups shredded cooked chicken

2 (14-ounce) cans artichoke hearts, drained, rinsed, and chopped

1 cup (4 ounces) shredded mozzarella cheese

4 slices cooked bacon, crumbled

½ cup sun-dried tomatoes, drained and chopped

2 (9-ounce) packages vegetable lasagna or 1 (10-ounce) package gluten-free oven-ready lasagna noodles

1 cup (4 ounces) shredded mozzarella cheese

½ cup (2 ounces) shredded or grated Parmesan cheese

PREHEAT THE OVEN to 375°F. Lightly grease a 13 x 9-inch baking dish.

MAKE THE KETO CREAM CHEESE SAUCE: Heat the cream and milk in a saucepan over medium. Stir in the garlic powder, salt, black pepper, nutmeg, and cayenne. Add the cream cheese and cook, stirring frequently, until the cheese melts and the mixture is smooth. Stir in the basil.

MAKE THE CHICKEN-ARTICHOKE FILLING: Combine the chicken, artichoke hearts, mozzarella, bacon, and sun-dried tomatoes in a large bowl.

ASSEMBLE: Spread about 1 cup cheese sauce in the bottom of the prepared dish and top evenly with one-third of the noodles. Top with one-third of the chicken filling and one-third of the cheese sauce. Repeat with the remaining noodles, chicken filling, and cheese sauce. Sprinkle the top with the mozzarella and Parmesan cheeses.

COVER AND BAKE for 30 minutes. Uncover and bake for 20 to 25 minutes until the lasagna is golden brown and bubbly. Let stand for 10 minutes before serving.

POULTRY

Romesco Grilled Chicken & Zucchini Lasagna

Romesco is a Spanish red sauce made with tomatoes and roasted red bell peppers that is usually served over grilled fish or chicken. (It also makes a nice additional dip to your crudité platters!) Here, the zesty sauce is interpreted into a layered lasagna entrée. Check the oven-ready noodles with a knife and let the dish bake five or ten additional minutes if they are not tender.

~~~~~~~~ **SERVES 4** ~~~~~~~~

ROMESCO SAUCE

- 2 large roasted red bell peppers, fresh roasted or jarred and drained well
- 1 (15-ounce) can fire-roasted diced tomatoes, undrained
- ¼ cup extra-virgin olive oil
- 2 tablespoons sherry vinegar
- 1 garlic clove, coarsely chopped
- ½ teaspoon fine sea salt
- ½ teaspoon freshly ground pepper
- ¼ teaspoon smoked paprika
- ½ cup silvered almonds, toasted

GRILLED CHICKEN & VEGETABLES

- 2 tablespoons extra-virgin olive oil
- 1 pound chicken cutlets
- 2 zucchini, cut lengthwise into ¼-inch strips
- ½ onion, sliced ¼-inch thick

- 6 to 8 oven-ready lasagna noodles
- 1 cup (4 ounces) shredded mozzarella
- 1 cup (4 ounces) shredded or grated Parmesan cheese
- 2 tablespoons sliced kalamata olives

PREHEAT THE GRILL to medium-high and the oven to 375°F. Lightly grease an 8 x 8-inch baking dish.

MAKE THE ROMESCO SAUCE: Combine the bell peppers, tomatoes, olive oil, vinegar, garlic, salt, pepper, and paprika in a blender. Process for 5 to 10 seconds or until well blended. Add the almonds, and pulse several times or until well blended. Set aside.

MAKE THE GRILLED CHICKEN & VEGETABLES: Brush the oil over the chicken, zucchini, and onion. Grill for 5 minutes on each side or until the chicken is done and the vegetables are tender. Cut the chicken into strips.

ASSEMBLE: Cover the bottom of the baking dish with ½ cup of the Romesco sauce. Top with 3 to 4 noodles, breaking to fit the pan. Top the noodles with half of the sauce, half of the chicken and vegetable mixture, and half of the mozzarella and Parmesan cheeses. Repeat with the remaining noodles, sauce, chicken and vegetable mixture, and cheeses. Sprinkle with the olives.

COVER AND BAKE for 35 minutes. Uncover and bake for 10 minutes. Let stand for 15 minutes before slicing.

Chicken & Asparagus Lasagna

When spring arrives and fresh asparagus is lined up in grocery stores (at a great price!), I will include it in any meal. This recipe suggests two pounds, but it works fine with just a single bunch. Winter spears tend to be thicker, and you may need to trim a bit more of the tough ends off the bottom. I suggest using a serrated knife to get through some of the fiber or chop the asparagus into one- and two-inch lengths before assembling for a fork-only entrée.

SERVES 6 TO 8

- 2 (1-pound) bunches fresh asparagus
- 2 tablespoons extra-virgin olive oil
- ¼ teaspoon fine sea salt
- ⅛ teaspoon freshly ground black pepper

SHALLOT SAUCE

- 3 tablespoons butter
- 2 shallots, minced
- 3 tablespoons all-purpose flour
- 2 cups chicken broth
- 1 cup heavy cream or half and half
- ½ teaspoon fine sea salt
- ½ cup (2 ounces) shredded Romano or Parmesan cheese

LEMON-RICOTTA FILLING

- 1 (15-ounce) container ricotta cheese
- 1 large egg
- ¼ teaspoon lemon zest
- 1 tablespoon fresh lemon juice
- ¼ teaspoon fine sea salt

- 8 oven-ready lasagna noodles
- 3 cups shredded or chopped rotisserie or cooked chicken
- 1 cup (4 ounces) shredded mozzarella or Italian blend cheese
- ½ cup (2 ounces) shredded or grated Romano or Parmesan cheese
- ¼ cup seasoned panko breadcrumbs

PREHEAT THE OVEN to 375°F. Lightly grease a 13 x 9-inch baking dish.

TRIM THE ASPARAGUS and place in a rimmed sheet pan. Drizzle with the olive oil and sprinkle with salt and pepper. Roll the asparagus to coat. Bake for 20 minutes or until tender.

MAKE THE SHALLOT SAUCE: Melt the butter in a large skillet over medium heat. Add the shallots and cook, stirring frequently, for 5 minutes or until tender. Whisk in the flour and cook, stirring constantly, for 1 minute. Whisk in the broth, cream, and salt. Cook, stirring frequently, for 5 to 7 minutes or until thickened. Add the Romano, stirring until smooth.

PREPARE THE LEMON-RICOTTA FILLING: Combine the ricotta, egg, lemon zest and juice, and salt in a bowl.

ASSEMBLE: Spread ½ cup of the shallot sauce in the bottom of the prepared dish. Top with 4 noodles, breaking to fit. Top the noodles with one-third of the sauce, half the chicken, and half of the ricotta filling. Arrange half of the asparagus over the ricotta. Repeat in this order: 4 noodles, one-third of the sauce, remaining chicken, ricotta, and asparagus. Spread the remaining sauce over the asparagus. Sprinkle with the mozzarella, Romano, and panko.

COVER AND BAKE for 30 minutes. Uncover and broil for 3 to 5 minutes or until golden brown and bubbly. Let stand for 10 minutes before serving.

Chicken-Ricotta Roll-Up Lasagna

Turn traditional layered lasagna around by rolling the cheesy ricotta filling inside the noodle. Ground chicken or turkey is usually pretty bland, so a bit of bacon in the pasta sauce adds some smoky flavor. You can substitute seasoned sun-dried tomatoes not packed in oil, but use very fresh (soft) ones as they tend to harden with age.

SERVES 6

12 lasagna noodles

CHICKEN-PEPPER PASTA SAUCE

2 tablespoons extra-virgin olive oil

⅛ teaspoon crushed red chili flakes

1 onion, chopped

1 red, yellow, or orange bell pepper, chopped

3 garlic cloves, minced

1 pound ground chicken or turkey

3 slices bacon, chopped

2 teaspoons Italian seasoning

1 (24-ounce) jar pasta or marinara sauce

½ teaspoon fine sea salt

¼ teaspoon freshly ground black pepper

SUN-DRIED TOMATO FILLING

1 (15-ounce) container ricotta cheese

1 cup (4 ounces) shredded mozzarella

½ cup oil-packed and seasoned sun-dried tomatoes, chopped

1 large egg

¼ cup chopped fresh basil

¼ teaspoon fine sea salt

1 cup (4 ounces) shredded or grated Parmesan cheese

PREHEAT THE OVEN to 350°F. Lightly grease a 13 x 9-inch baking dish.

COOK THE LASAGNA NOODLES in boiling salted water according to the package directions. Drain, then rinse in cool water.

MAKE THE CHICKEN-PEPPER PASTA SAUCE: Heat the oil in a large skillet over medium-high. Add the chili flakes, onion, bell pepper, and garlic. Cook, stirring frequently, for 7 to 10 minutes or until the vegetables are tender. Add the ground chicken, bacon, and Italian seasoning. Cook, stirring frequently, or until the meat is browned and crumbled. Add the pasta sauce, salt, and pepper. Cook, stirring occasionally, for 15 minutes or until the sauce thickens.

MAKE THE SUN-DRIED TOMATO FILLING: Combine the ricotta, mozzarella, sun-dried tomatoes, egg, basil, and salt in a medium bowl.

ASSEMBLE: Spoon 2 cups of the sauce in the bottom of the prepared baking dish. Place the noodles flat on a work surface. Spread about ⅓ cup of the ricotta cheese filling in the center of the noodle and roll both the top and bottom of the noodles onto each other. Place the roll ups, seam side down, in the baking dish. Repeat with the remaining noodles and filling. Spoon the remaining sauce over the roll ups. Sprinkle with the Parmesan cheese.

COVER AND BAKE for 30 minutes. Uncover and bake for 15 minutes until golden brown and bubbly. Let stand for 10 minutes before serving.

Chicken Piccata Ricotta Lasagna

Capers provide a pungent, salty flavor featured in this lemony butter sauce. It's recommended to rinse and drain the tiny buds to remove excess brine. You may see "nonpareil" on the label. Capers are sorted by size, and that term just means they are the smallest.

SERVES 8

CAPER WHITE SAUCE

- 2 tablespoons butter
- 1 shallot, minced
- 3 tablespoons all-purpose flour
- ½ cup white wine
- 2 cups chicken broth
- ½ cup half and half or heavy cream
- 1½ tablespoons fresh lemon juice
- 1 tablespoon capers, rinsed and drained

LEMON RICOTTA FILLING

- 1 (15-ounce) container ricotta cheese
- 1 large egg
- 1 cup (4 ounces) shredded mozzarella cheese
- ½ teaspoon lemon zest
- ¼ cup chopped fresh Italian parsley

- 8 to 10 oven-ready lasagna noodles
- 3 cups shredded or chopped rotisserie or cooked chicken
- 1 cup (4 ounces) shredded or grated Parmesan cheese
- 1 lemon, very thinly sliced (optional)

PREHEAT THE OVEN to 350°F. Lightly grease a 13 x 9-inch baking dish.

MAKE THE CAPER WHITE SAUCE: Melt the butter in a large skillet over medium-high heat. Add the shallot and cook, stirring constantly, for 3 minutes. Whisk in the flour and cook, stirring constantly, for 1 minute. Whisk in the wine and cook for 1 to 2 minutes, until the liquid evaporates. Whisk in the chicken broth and half and half. Cook, stirring frequently, for 5 minutes or until thickened. Stir in the lemon juice and capers.

MAKE THE LEMON RICOTTA FILLING: Combine the ricotta, egg, mozzarella, lemon zest, and parsley in a bowl.

ASSEMBLE: Spread ½ cup of the white sauce in the bottom of the prepared dish. Top with 4 to 5 noodles, breaking to fit. Spread with ½ cup of the sauce, half of the ricotta filling, and half of the chicken. Repeat with the remaining noodles, ½ cup sauce, remaining ricotta filling, and the rest of the chicken. Pour the remaining sauce over the chicken. Sprinkle the top evenly with the Parmesan cheese. Arrange the lemon slices on top, if using.

COVER AND BAKE for 40 minutes. (Check with a knife to make sure the noodles are tender.) Uncover and broil for 3 to 5 minutes until golden brown and bubbly. Let stand 10 minutes before serving.

POULTRY

Roasted Broccoli & Chicken Lasagna

Be sure to roast the broccoli until the edges are dark brown and very lightly charred. This extra step is worth it since it adds a lot of flavor. The bottom of the florets will brown if they are touching the baking sheet, so cut them in half and place them cut side down for maximum contact. Rotisserie chicken is usually very tender, but you can bake chicken breasts (two to three) or thighs (four to six), if preferred. Double the oil, salt, and garlic powder to ensure the chicken is properly seasoned. Cut the breasts in half lengthwise to create cutlets that will finish baking by the time the broccoli is tender.

SERVES 6 TO 8

12 lasagna noodles

ROASTED BROCCOLI
& CHICKEN FILLING

2 tablespoons extra-virgin olive oil

¾ teaspoons fine sea salt

½ teaspoon garlic powder

6 cups fresh broccoli florets

4 cups shredded rotisserie or chopped cooked chicken meat

GREEN ONION
BÉCHAMEL SAUCE

3 tablespoons butter

3 tablespoons all-purpose flour

2 cups chicken or vegetable broth

1 cup heavy cream

1 cup (4 ounces) shredded cheddar cheese

3 green onions, chopped

½ teaspoon fine sea salt

¼ teaspoon freshly ground black pepper

1 cup (4 ounces) shredded cheddar cheese

1 cup (4 ounces) shredded Asiago or Parmesan cheese

¼ cup crushed butter crackers or panko breadcrumbs

PREHEAT THE OVEN to 425°F. Line a baking sheet with nonstick foil. Lightly grease a 13 x 9-inch baking dish.

COOK THE LASAGNA NOODLES in boiling salted water according to the package directions. Drain, then rinse in cool water.

MAKE THE ROASTED BROCCOLI AND CHICKEN FILLING: Combine the oil, salt, and garlic powder in a large bowl. Add the broccoli, tossing to coat. Spread the broccoli in an even layer on the baking sheet. Bake for 20 minutes until the broccoli is tender and browned on the edges. Return the broccoli to the bowl and stir in the chicken. Reduce the oven temperature to 375°F.

MAKE THE GREEN ONION BÉCHAMEL SAUCE: Melt the butter in a large saucepan over medium-high heat. Whisk in the flour and cook, stirring constantly, for 1 minute. Whisk in the broth and cream. Cook, stirring frequently, for 5 minutes or until the mixture thickens. Stir in the cheddar cheese, then add the green onions, salt, and black pepper, stirring to combine.

ASSEMBLE: Spread ½ cup of the sauce in the bottom of the prepared dish. Top with 3 noodles. Spoon in one-third of the sauce, one-third of the chicken-broccoli filling, and one-third of the cheddar cheese. Repeat twice in this order: noodles, sauce, chicken filling, and cheddar cheese. Sprinkle the top evenly with the Asiago and panko.

COVER AND BAKE for 30 minutes. Uncover and bake for 20 minutes until golden brown and bubbly. Let stand for 10 minutes before serving.

Chicken Alfredo & Arugula Pesto Lasagna

While traditional pesto is made with fresh basil, I enjoy variations using arugula, spinach, watercress, cilantro, or any other pungent green lettuce or herb. I always add fresh lemon since it keeps the color bright while keeping the fresh sauce from tasting heavy.

~~~~~~~~~~ **SERVES 8** ~~~~~~~~~~

9 lasagna noodles

ARUGULA-WALNUT PESTO

1 (5-ounce) container baby arugula

1 large garlic clove, minced

¾ cup (3 ounces) shredded or grated Parmesan cheese

⅔ cup extra-virgin olive oil

2 tablespoons fresh lemon juice

½ teaspoon fine sea salt

½ cup toasted walnuts

1 (24-ounce) jar pasta or marinara sauce

3 cups shredded or chopped rotisserie or cooked chicken

1 (15-ounce) container refrigerated Alfredo sauce or 1½ cups jarred

1 cup (4 ounces) shredded mozzarella cheese

PREHEAT THE OVEN to 350°F. Lightly grease a 13 x 9-inch baking dish.

COOK THE NOODLES in boiling salted water according to the package directions. Drain, then rinse in cool water.

MAKE THE ARUGULA-WALNUT PESTO: Combine the arugula, garlic, Parmesan, olive oil, lemon juice, and salt in a food processor. Pulse until finely chopped. Add the walnuts and pulse until finely chopped.

ASSEMBLE: Spread ¾ cup of the pasta sauce in the bottom of the prepared baking dish. Top with 3 noodles. Spread one-third of the chicken and all of the pesto over the noodles. Layer with 3 noodles, one-third of the chicken, and the remaining pasta sauce. Top with the remaining 3 noodles, remaining chicken, and all of the Alfredo sauce. Sprinkle with the mozzarella cheese.

COVER AND BAKE for 30 minutes. Uncover and bake for 15 minutes until golden brown and bubbly. Let stand for 10 minutes before serving.

Chicken & Caramelized Onion Lasagna with Blue Cheese Béchamel

This unique combination works for people who love rich umami flavors. Any type of blue cheese works—Danish, Gorgonzola, Roquefort—so pick your favorite. Patience is required for making caramelized onions, and the sweet earthy flavor is worth the time. The good news is that they don't require a lot of babysitting. Do pay attention the last five minutes of cooking and stir a bit more frequently to make sure the onions don't burn.

SERVES 6

CHICKEN & ONION FILLING

3 tablespoons butter

4 onions, quartered and sliced

¼ teaspoon fine sea salt

3 cups shredded or chopped rotisserie chicken

½ cup toasted walnuts, coarsely chopped

BLUE CHEESE BÉCHAMEL SAUCE

2 tablespoons butter

2 tablespoons all-purpose flour

1 cup chicken or vegetable broth

1 cup half and half or whole milk

½ to ¾ cup (2 to 3 ounces) crumbled blue cheese

6 oven-ready lasagna noodles

⅓ cup (1½ ounces) shredded or grated Parmesan cheese

MAKE THE CHICKEN AND ONION FILLING: Melt the butter in a large skillet over medium-low heat. Add the onions and salt. Cover and cook, stirring frequently, for 10 minutes until the onions are translucent. Uncover and cook for 35 to 40 minutes, stirring occasionally, or until golden brown. Transfer to a bowl. Stir in the chicken and walnuts.

PREHEAT THE OVEN to 375°F. Lightly grease an 8 x 8-inch baking dish.

MAKE THE BLUE CHEESE BÉCHAMEL SAUCE: Melt the butter in a large skillet over medium-high heat. Whisk in the flour and cook, stirring constantly, for 1 minute. Whisk in the broth and half and half. Cook, stirring frequently, for 5 minutes or until thickened. Add the blue cheese, stirring until smooth.

ASSEMBLE: Spread ¼ cup of the blue cheese sauce in the bottom of the prepared dish and top with 2 noodles. Layer in this order: ¼ cup sauce, half of the chicken mixture, 2 noodles, ¼ cup sauce, remaining chicken mixture, remaining 2 noodles. Spread the remaining sauce over the lasagna and sprinkle evenly with the Parmesan cheese.

COVER AND BAKE for 40 minutes until golden brown and bubbly. Let stand for 10 minutes before serving.

POULTRY

Roasted Butternut Squash & Chicken Lasagna

Aside from an earthy flavor and loads of nutrition, winter squash has a long shelf life, so you can store it for a few weeks to be ready when the craving strikes. If the squash is tough and difficult to peel or cut, microwave it on high for one minute to soften the rind. The recipe is pretty forgiving about the size of the butternut, so a little under or over will still work just fine.

SERVES 8

CHICKEN–BUTTERNUT SQUASH FILLING

- 1 (2 to 2½ pound) butternut squash (about 6 cups diced)
- 2 tablespoons extra-virgin olive oil
- ½ teaspoon fine sea salt
- ½ teaspoon freshly ground black pepper
- 1 tablespoon chopped fresh rosemary
- 5 slices lean bacon
- 3 cups shredded rotisserie or cooked chicken

- 8 lasagna noodles

PARMESAN-SAGE BÉCHAMEL SAUCE

- 2 tablespoons butter
- 2 tablespoons all-purpose flour
- 2½ cups half and half or milk
- ½ teaspoon fine sea salt
- ¼ teaspoon ground sage
- ½ cup (2 ounces) shredded or grated Parmesan cheese

- 1 cup (4 ounces) shredded or grated Parmesan cheese
- ½ cup chopped walnuts
- 2 tablespoons chopped fresh Italian parsley

PREHEAT THE OVEN to 400°F. Line a rimmed sheet pan with foil. Lightly grease a 13 x 9-inch baking dish.

MAKE THE CHICKEN–BUTTERNUT SQUASH FILLING: Peel, seed, and cut the squash into cubes. Place in a large bowl and add the oil, salt, pepper, and rosemary, tossing to coat. Spread the squash out evenly on the sheet pan. Place the bacon in an even layer on one side (the strips might fit better if cut in half or in pieces). Bake, occasionally stirring the squash and flipping the bacon, for 30 minutes or until the squash is just tender and the bacon crisp. Coarsely chop or crumble the bacon. Combine the butternut squash, bacon, and chicken in a large bowl.

COOK THE LASAGNA NOODLES in boiling salted water according to the package directions. Drain, then rinse in cool water.

PREPARE THE PARMESAN-SAGE BÉCHAMEL SAUCE: Melt the butter in a large skillet over medium-high heat. Whisk in the flour and cook, stirring constantly, for 1 minute. Whisk in the half and half, salt, and sage. Cook, stirring frequently, for 5 minutes or until the mixture thickens. Add the Parmesan and cook, stirring occasionally, until the sauce is smooth.

ASSEMBLE: Spread ½ cup of the béchamel sauce in the bottom of the prepared baking dish and top with 4 noodles. Top the noodles with half of the squash filling and half of the béchamel sauce. Repeat with the noodles, squash filling, and sauce. Sprinkle the top with the Parmesan cheese and walnuts.

COVER AND BAKE for 30 minutes. Uncover and bake for 15 minutes until golden brown and bubbly. Let stand for 10 minutes before serving. Sprinkle with the parsley.

POULTRY

79

Slow Cooker Parmesan-Garlic Chicken

You have lots of choices with the added vegetable—try julienned carrots, broccoli florets, thawed and drained frozen spinach, baby or English peas, chopped asparagus, or chopped zucchini or yellow squash. Many slow cooker recipes include cooking on low heat at six to eight hours, but this one is ready in less time. Remember to set your timer to avoid overcooking.

~~~~~~~~~~~~~~ **SERVES 6** ~~~~~~~~~~~~~~

PARMESAN-GARLIC
BÉCHAMEL SAUCE

3 tablespoons butter

5 garlic cloves, minced

3 tablespoons all-purpose flour

3 cups half and half or whole milk

½ teaspoon fine sea salt

¼ teaspoon ground nutmeg

1 cup (4 ounces) shredded or grated Parmesan cheese

9 lasagna noodles

3 cups shredded or chopped rotisserie or cooked chicken

2 cups mixed vegetables, cut into bite-size pieces

1 cup (4 ounces) shredded mozzarella or Italian blend cheese

MAKE THE PARMESAN-GARLIC BÉCHAMEL SAUCE:
Melt the butter in a large skillet over medium-low heat. Add the garlic and cook, stirring frequently, for 3 minutes, or until the garlic is tender but not browned. Whisk in the flour and cook, stirring constantly, for 1 minute. Whisk in the half and half, salt, and nutmeg. Cook, stirring frequently, for 5 to 7 minutes or until thickened. Add the Parmesan and cook, stirring occasionally, until the sauce is smooth.

ASSEMBLE: Lightly grease the inside of a 4-quart slow cooker. Pour 1 cup of the béchamel sauce into the bottom of the slow cooker. Cover the sauce with 3 noodles, breaking them to fit in an even layer. Top with one-third of the chicken, one-third of the vegetables, and one-third of the sauce. Repeat twice with the remaining noodles, chicken, vegetables, and sauce. Sprinkle with the mozzarella cheese.

COVER THE SLOW COOKER
and cook on low for 4 hours. Insert a knife into the lasagna to make sure the noodles are soft. Let stand for 10 minutes before serving.

80

Chicken Cordon Bleu Lasagna Rolls

Ham and chicken rolled up into neat bundles and draped in a cheesy white sauce makes a company-worthy dish. To keep the bundles neat, place the ham and the chicken over most of the ricotta, leaving about two inches of the noodle spread with just the ricotta. That'll make the seams flatten and keep the rolls steady.

〜〜〜〜〜〜〜 **SERVES 6** 〜〜〜〜〜〜〜

12 lasagna noodles

SWISS WHITE SAUCE

2 tablespoons butter

2 tablespoons all-purpose flour

1 cup chicken broth

2 cups half and half or whole milk

1 cup (4 ounces) shredded Swiss or Gruyére cheese

¼ teaspoon ground nutmeg

RICOTTA FILLING

1 (15-ounce) container ricotta cheese

1 large egg

1 cup (4 ounces) shredded Swiss cheese

¼ teaspoon fine sea salt

¼ teaspoon freshly ground black pepper

8 ounces very thin sliced deli ham, sliced into 2-inch-wide pieces

3 cups shredded or chopped rotisserie chicken

1½ tablespoons melted butter

½ cup Italian-seasoned panko breadcrumbs

¼ cup (1 ounce) grated Parmesan cheese

PREHEAT THE OVEN to 350°F. Lightly grease a 13 x 9-inch baking dish.

COOK THE LASAGNA NOODLES in boiling salted water according to the package directions. Drain, then rinse in cool water.

MAKE THE SWISS WHITE SAUCE: Melt the butter in a large skillet over medium-high heat. Whisk in the flour and cook, stirring constantly, for 1 minute. Whisk in the broth and half and half and cook, stirring frequently, for 5 minutes or until thickened. Add the Swiss cheese and nutmeg, stirring until smooth.

MAKE THE RICOTTA FILLING: Combine the ricotta, egg, Swiss cheese, salt, and pepper in a bowl.

ASSEMBLE: Spread 1 cup of the white sauce in the bottom of the prepared dish. Lay out the lasagna noodles on a flat surface. Spread each one with about 3 tablespoons of the ricotta mixture. Place a slice of ham over the ricotta and sprinkle with ¼ cup of shredded chicken. Roll up and place, seam side down, in the prepared dish. Repeat with remaining noodles, ricotta, ham, and chicken. Pour the remaining sauce over the lasagna rolls.

COMBINE THE MELTED BUTTER, panko, and Parmesan cheese in a small bowl. Sprinkle over the lasagna.

COVER AND BAKE for 40 minutes or until golden brown and bubbly. Uncover and bake for 20 minutes. Let stand for 10 minutes before serving.

POULTRY

Roasted Garlic, Chicken & Sweet Potato Lasagna

Roasting whole heads of garlic is culinary magic. What is usually a sharp, pungent flavor mellows with heat and time into something smooth and rich. You can roast it right before using, but since roasted garlic can be made up to a week ahead, I'll pop in a foil package of garlic whenever I've got the oven going. Stir the mashed garlic into any type of sauce or gravy, as well as soups, salad dressings, hummus, and so on.

~~~ **SERVES 8** ~~~

ROASTED GARLIC BÉCHAMEL SAUCE

- 1 large head garlic
- 1 tablespoon extra-virgin olive oil
- 2 tablespoons butter
- 2 tablespoons all-purpose flour
- 2½ cups heavy cream or half and half
- ¼ teaspoon fine sea salt
- ¼ teaspoon freshly ground black pepper
- ½ cup (2 ounces) shredded Parmesan cheese

RICOTTA FILLING

- 2 (15-ounce) containers ricotta cheese
- 2 large eggs
- ½ teaspoon fine sea salt
- ½ teaspoon freshly ground black pepper

SWEET POTATO– CHICKEN FILLING

- 1 tablespoon extra-virgin olive oil
- 1 sweet potato, peeled and finely chopped
- ½ onion, finely chopped
- 1 teaspoon fresh thyme leaves
- 3 cups shredded or chopped cooked chicken

- 16 oven-ready lasagna noodles
- 1 cup (4 ounces) shredded mozzarella or Parmesan cheese

PREHEAT THE OVEN to 375°F. Lightly grease a 13 x 9-inch baking dish.

MAKE THE ROASTED GARLIC BÉCHAMEL SAUCE: Cut off the top or pointed end of the garlic head, removing the loose, papery skin (do not completely peel or separate the cloves). Place the garlic head on a large piece of foil, cut side up, and drizzle with the oil. Wrap the foil tightly around the garlic and bake for 45 to 50 minutes or until the garlic is soft. Remove the garlic from the oven and let stand until cool enough to handle. Squeeze the pulp from the garlic head, discarding tough skins. Place in a bowl and mash until smooth. Set aside.

MELT THE BUTTER in a large skillet over medium-high heat. Whisk in the flour and cook, stirring constantly, for 1 minute. Whisk in the cream, mashed garlic, salt, and pepper. Cook, stirring frequently, for 5 minutes or until the mixture thickens. Add the Parmesan and cook, stirring occasionally, until the sauce is smooth.

PREPARE THE RICOTTA FILLING: Combine the ricotta cheese, eggs, salt, and pepper in a small bowl.

MAKE THE SWEET POTATO– CHICKEN FILLING: Heat the olive oil in a large skillet over medium-high. Add the sweet potato, onion, and thyme. Cook, stirring frequently, until the vegetables are tender. Stir in the chicken.

ASSEMBLE: Spoon ½ cup of the béchamel sauce into the bottom of the prepared dish. Top with 4 noodles, breaking to fit the dish. Layer in this order: ½ cup béchamel sauce, half of the chicken, 4 noodles, all of the ricotta, 4 noodles, ½ cup sauce, remaining chicken, 4 noodles, and the remaining sauce. Sprinkle with the mozzarella.

COVER AND BAKE for 40 minutes. Uncover and bake for 10 minutes or until golden brown and bubbly. Let stand for 10 minutes before serving.

POULTRY

Mexican Chicken, Black Bean & Corn Lasagna

Jalapeños vary in heat, but most of the fire comes from the interior ribs and seeds. It's said that the ones with small brown lines, called corking, are particularly spicy. Those lines are the equivalent of stretch marks and indicate a mature pepper. Generally, the older the pepper, the hotter it is. Use gloves when mincing, or wash your hands thoroughly after prep to remove the volatile oils.

~~~ **SERVES 8** ~~~

1 tablespoon extra-virgin olive oil

½ red onion, chopped

1 jalapeño, seeded and minced

2 garlic cloves, minced

1 tablespoon chili powder

1 teaspoon ground cumin

¾ teaspoon fine sea salt

1 pound ground chicken

1 (15-ounce) can black or pinto beans, rinsed and drained

1 (15-ounce) can corn kernels, drained, or 1¼ cups frozen corn, thawed

1 (14.5-ounce) can chili-seasoned diced tomatoes, undrained

1 (8-ounce) can tomato sauce

¼ cup chopped fresh cilantro

12 (4-inch) corn tortillas

2 cups (8 ounces) shredded Monterey Jack, Pepper Jack, or Mexican-flavored cheese blend

1 tomato, seeded and finely chopped

1 avocado, diced

PREHEAT THE OVEN to 350°F. Lightly grease a 13 x 9-inch baking dish.

HEAT THE OIL in a large nonstick skillet over medium-high. Add the onion, jalapeño, garlic, chili powder, cumin, and salt. Cook, stirring occasionally, for 5 minutes or until the onion is tender. Add the chicken and cook for 10 minutes or until browned and crumbled. Stir in the beans, corn, diced tomatoes, and tomato sauce. Cook, stirring occasionally, for 15 minutes. Stir in the cilantro.

ASSEMBLE: Arrange half the tortillas in the bottom of the prepared dish, cutting some to fit in an even layer. Top with half the chicken mixture and half the cheese. Repeat with the remaining tortillas, chicken mixture, and cheese.

COVER AND BAKE for 20 minutes. Uncover and bake for 10 minutes or until golden brown and bubbly. Let stand for 10 minutes before serving. Sprinkle with the tomato and avocado.

Winter Squash
Marinara & Ricotta Lasagna

Cooked squash puree makes an interesting and healthful twist to a lasagna. The frozen bricks will probably be a mix of butternut and acorn or some variation of winter squash. Frozen and thawed squash tends to be watery, but a few minutes simmering on the cooktop will transform it into a thick sauce. Another option is canned pumpkin, which, surprisingly, might also contain other winter squash. Either way, winter squash is considered a superfood with loads of carotenoids, vitamins, minerals, and fiber.

~~~~~~~~~~ **SERVES 8** ~~~~~~~~~~

WINTER SQUASH MARINARA

1 tablespoon extra-virgin olive oil

1 pound ground turkey or turkey sausage

¼ cup white wine or chicken broth

1 cup pasta or marinara sauce

2 (15-ounce) cans pumpkin puree or 2 (12-ounce) packages frozen squash puree

¾ teaspoon ground cumin

¾ teaspoon fine sea salt

½ teaspoon ground cinnamon

RICOTTA-FETA FILLING

1 (15-ounce) container ricotta cheese

1 cup (4 ounces) crumbled feta, soft goat, or shredded Parmesan cheese

1 large egg

½ teaspoon freshly ground black pepper

8 to 10 oven-ready lasagna noodles

1 cup (4 ounces) shredded Gruyère, Havarti, or mozzarella cheese

½ cup (2 ounces) shredded or grated Parmesan cheese

PREHEAT THE OVEN to 375°F. Lightly grease a 13 x 9-inch baking dish.

MAKE THE WINTER SQUASH MARINARA: Heat the oil in a large skillet over medium-high. Add the turkey and cook, stirring frequently, for 5 minutes or until browned. Add the wine and cook, stirring constantly, for 1 minute, scraping the bottom of the skillet to loosen any browned bits. Stir in the pasta sauce, squash puree, cumin, salt, and cinnamon. Cook, stirring occasionally, for 5 minutes or until the sauce thickens.

MAKE THE RICOTTA-FETA FILLING: Combine the ricotta, feta, egg, and pepper in a bowl.

ASSEMBLE: Spread about 1 cup of the marinara sauce in the bottom of the prepared dish and top with 4 to 5 lasagna noodles, breaking pieces to fit if needed. Spread with half of the ricotta filling and half of the sauce. Repeat with the remaining noodles, ricotta, and sauce. Sprinkle with the Gruyère and Parmesan cheeses.

COVER AND BAKE for 40 minutes. Uncover and bake for 10 minutes or until golden brown. Let stand for 10 minutes before serving.

Turkey Pot Pie Lasagna

Saucy pot pies and noodle soups make excellent comfort foods, and this lasagna gets its inspiration from these homey flavors. If you want to add more green vegetables into the meal, stir a cup of frozen green peas (thawed) into the sauce after it has thickened.

SERVES 8

VEGGIE WHITE SAUCE

4 tablespoons butter

1 onion, chopped

4 carrots, finely chopped

3 celery ribs, finely chopped

3 garlic cloves, minced

¼ cup all-purpose flour

2 cups chicken or turkey broth

2 cups half and half or whole milk

1 teaspoon poultry seasoning

¾ teaspoon fine sea salt

9 to 12 oven-ready lasagna noodles

3¾ cups shredded or chopped cooked turkey or chicken

1½ cups (6 ounces) shredded Swiss cheese

1 cup (4 ounces) shredded or grated Parmesan cheese

½ cup cracker or panko crumbs

PREHEAT THE OVEN to 350°F. Lightly grease a 13 x 9-inch baking dish.

MAKE THE VEGGIE WHITE SAUCE: Melt the butter in a large skillet over medium-high heat. Add the onion, carrots, celery, and garlic. Cook, stirring frequently, for 7 to 10 minutes or until the vegetables are tender. Stir in the flour and cook, stirring constantly, for 1 minute. Stir in the broth, half and half, poultry seasoning, and salt. Cook, stirring frequently, for 5 minutes or until the sauce thickens.

ASSEMBLE: Spoon 1½ cups of the sauce in the bottom of the prepared baking dish. Arrange 3 to 4 noodles over the sauce, breaking to fit the pan. Spread one-third of the turkey, one-third of the Swiss cheese, and one-third of the white sauce over the noodles. Repeat twice in this order: noodles, turkey, Swiss, and sauce. Sprinkle with the Parmesan cheese and cracker crumbs.

COVER AND BAKE for 40 minutes. Uncover and bake for 15 minutes or until golden brown and bubbly. Let stand for 10 minutes before serving.

POULTRY

Keto-Friendly Turkey Sausage & Kale Lasagna

In the specialty-diet section of your grocery store, look for keto options such as vegetable lasagna noodles made from hearts of palm. Gluten-free noodles are made from high-carb corn and rice, so if you can't find the specialty noodles, you can slice zucchini planks.

SERVES 8

- 1 tablespoon extra-virgin olive oil
- 1 (8- to 10-ounce) package cremini or button mushrooms, sliced
- ½ teaspoon fine sea salt
- ½ teaspoon freshly ground black pepper
- 1 (5-ounce) container baby kale (6 cups)

TURKEY SAUSAGE SAUCE

- 1 tablespoon extra-virgin olive oil
- 1 onion, chopped
- 1 pound ground turkey
- 8 ounces turkey sausage, casings removed
- ¼ teaspoon crushed red pepper flakes
- 1 (24-ounce) jar no-sugar-added pasta sauce

BASIL, GOAT CHEESE & RICOTTA FILLING

- 2 (15-ounce) containers ricotta cheese
- 4 to 6 ounces soft goat cheese
- 2 large eggs
- 2 tablespoons chopped fresh basil
- ¼ teaspoon fine sea salt
- ¼ teaspoon freshly ground black pepper

- 1 (9-ounce) package oven-ready vegetable lasagna noodles
- 8 ounces fresh mozzarella, cut into pieces, or 2 cups shredded mozzarella

PREHEAT THE OVEN to 350°F. Lightly grease a 13 x 9-inch baking dish.

HEAT THE OLIVE OIL in a large skillet over medium-high. Add the mushrooms, salt, and pepper and cook, stirring occasionally, for 5 to 7 minutes or until tender. Add the kale and cook, tossing with tongs, for 5 minutes or until the kale wilts. Transfer to a bowl.

MAKE THE TURKEY SAUSAGE SAUCE: Heat the oil in a large skillet over medium. Add the onion and cook, stirring occasionally, for 5 to 7 minutes or until tender. Add the ground turkey, turkey sausage, and red pepper flakes. Cook, stirring frequently, for 10 minutes until the meat is browned and crumbly. Stir in the pasta sauce.

MAKE THE RICOTTA FILLING: Combine the ricotta, goat cheese, eggs, basil, salt, and pepper in a bowl.

ASSEMBLE: Spread 1 cup of the sausage sauce in the bottom of the prepared dish. Top with half of the noodles. Spread with half of the ricotta filling, half of the sausage sauce, and all of the mushroom-kale mixture. Top with the remaining noodles, ricotta, and sausage sauce. Sprinkle with the mozzarella cheese.

BAKE, UNCOVERED, for 35 minutes. Broil for 3 to 5 minutes or until golden brown and bubbly. Let stand for 10 minutes before serving.

Roasted Fall Veggies & Turkey Lasagna

The earthy flavor of ripe Brie cheese pairs well with a bevy of roasted fall vegetables. Use either oil-packed or dry sun-dried tomatoes, but don't be surprised if the oil-packed ones cast a pink color to the sauce.

~ **SERVES 8** ~

ROASTED FALL VEGGIES

- 3 tablespoon extra-virgin olive oil
- 2 tablespoons chopped fresh rosemary
- ½ teaspoon fine sea salt
- 1 head cauliflower, cut into florets
- 1 sweet potato, peeled and sliced
- 1 (8- or 10-ounce) package cremini mushrooms, halved
- 2 carrots, sliced
- 1 sweet onion, thickly sliced

BRIE, BASIL & TOMATO WHITE SAUCE

- 2 tablespoons butter
- 2 tablespoons all-purpose flour
- 1½ cups half and half or whole milk
- 4 ounces Brie or goat cheese, or (1 cup) shredded or grated Parmesan cheese
- ½ cup chopped sun-dried tomatoes
- ¼ cup chopped fresh basil

RICOTTA FILLING

- 1 (15-ounce) container ricotta cheese
- 2 large eggs
- 1 cup (4 ounces) shredded Parmesan cheese
- ¼ teaspoon fine sea salt
- ¼ teaspoon freshly ground black pepper

- 10 oven-ready lasagna noodles
- 3 cups shredded cooked turkey or rotisserie chicken
- 1 cup (4 ounces) shredded or grated Parmesan cheese

PREHEAT THE OVEN to 425°F. Lightly grease a 13 x 9-inch baking dish.

MAKE THE ROASTED FALL VEGGIES: Combine the oil, rosemary, and salt in a large bowl. Add the cauliflower, sweet potato, mushrooms, carrots, and onion, tossing gently to coat. Transfer to a large rimmed sheet pan. Bake for 20 minutes, stirring occasionally, until the vegetables are tender and start to brown on the edges. Remove from the oven and reduce the temperature to 350°F.

MAKE THE BRIE, BASIL, AND TOMATO WHITE SAUCE: Melt the butter in a large skillet over medium-high heat. Whisk in the flour and cook, stirring constantly, for 1 minute. Whisk in the half and half and cook, stirring frequently, for 5 minutes or until thickened. Add the cheese, sun-dried tomatoes, and basil and cook, stirring occasionally, or until smooth.

ASSEMBLE: Spread ¾ cup of the white sauce in the bottom of the prepared dish. Top with 5 noodles. Layer half of the turkey, half of the vegetables, and half of the sauce over the noodles. Repeat with 5 noodles, the remaining turkey, vegetables, and sauce. Sprinkle with the Parmesan cheese.

COVER AND BAKE for 30 minutes. Uncover and bake for 10 minutes or until golden brown and bubbly. Let stand for 10 minutes before serving.

VEGETARIAN

Feta & Spinach Lasagna

Fans of spanakopita will enjoy this simple spinach and feta combo. I added a bit of lemon zest to give the spinach flavor a lift. During a retest, I ran out of feta (someone in my house had been nibbling the cheese!), so I substituted about a quarter cup of crumbled blue cheese. Yum—it made a delicious variation!

~~~~~~~~ **SERVES 8** ~~~~~~~~

SPINACH FILLING

- 1 tablespoon extra-virgin olive oil
- 1 onion, chopped
- ¼ teaspoon crushed red pepper flakes
- 4 garlic cloves, minced
- 2 (10-ounce) containers fresh baby spinach
- ¼ teaspoon fine sea salt
- ½ teaspoon freshly ground black pepper
- ¼ teaspoon lemon zest

PARMESAN BÉCHAMEL SAUCE

- 2 tablespoons butter
- 2 tablespoons all-purpose flour
- 2½ cups half and half or whole milk
- ½ teaspoon fine sea salt
- ¼ teaspoon ground nutmeg (optional)
- 1 cup (4 ounces) shredded or grated Parmesan cheese

- 9 oven-ready lasagna noodles
- 2 cups (8 ounces) feta cheese, crumbled
- ½ cup (2 ounces) shredded or grated Parmesan cheese
- ⅓ cup toasted sliced almonds

PREHEAT THE OVEN to 350°F. Lightly grease an 8 x 8-inch baking dish.

MAKE THE SPINACH FILLING: Heat the oil in a large skillet over medium-high. Add the onion and red pepper flakes and cook, stirring frequently, for 5 minutes or until the onion is tender. Add the garlic and cook, stirring constantly, for 1 minute. Add the spinach in batches, tossing and stirring with tongs until the spinach wilts. Stir in the salt, pepper, and lemon zest. If desired, transfer the spinach to a bowl to use the same skillet to prepare the sauce.

MAKE THE PARMESAN BÉCHAMEL SAUCE: Melt the butter in a large skillet over medium-high heat. Whisk in the flour and cook, stirring constantly, for 1 minute. Whisk in the half and half, salt, and nutmeg, if using. Cook, stirring frequently, for 5 minutes or until the mixture thickens. Add the Parmesan and cook, stirring occasionally, until the sauce is smooth.

ASSEMBLE: Spread ½ cup of the béchamel sauce in the bottom of the prepared baking dish. Top with 3 noodles, breaking the noodles to fit the dish. Top the noodles with one-third of the spinach, spreading it out with a fork. (The spinach might release excess water when standing. It's okay to use the flavorful liquid in the lasagna. If you used frozen spinach, there may be too much liquid, so use a slotted spoon.) Top the spinach with one-third of the remaining white sauce and one-third of the feta. Repeat twice in this order: noodles, spinach, sauce, and feta. Sprinkle the top with the Parmesan cheese and toasted almonds.

COVER AND BAKE for 40 minutes. Uncover and bake for 10 minutes until golden brown. Let stand for 10 minutes before serving.

Spinach & Artichoke Lasagna

Love spinach-artichoke dip? Then try this variation of the beloved appetizer. For heartier eaters, stir two cups of shredded rotisserie or grilled chicken into the artichoke mixture.

~~~ **SERVES 4 TO 6** ~~~

SPINACH-ARTICHOKE FILLING

- 1 (8-ounce) package cream cheese, softened
- 1 cup ricotta cheese
- ½ cup (2 ounces) shredded or grated Parmesan cheese
- ¼ cup mayonnaise
- 2 teaspoons Italian seasoning
- ¾ teaspoon fine sea salt
- ½ teaspoon freshly ground black pepper
- 1 (12-ounce) bag frozen spinach, thawed and drained well
- 1 (14-ounce) can artichoke hearts, drained and chopped

PARMESAN BÉCHAMEL SAUCE

- 4 tablespoons butter
- ⅛ teaspoon red pepper flakes
- ¼ cup all-purpose flour
- 2½ cups whole milk
- 1 cup (4 ounces) shredded or grated Parmesan cheese

- 9 oven-ready lasagna noodles
- 2 cups (8 ounces) shredded mozzarella cheese

PREHEAT THE OVEN to 375°F. Lightly grease a 9 x 9-inch or 8 x 8-inch baking dish.

MAKE THE SPINACH-ARTICHOKE FILLING: Stir together the cream cheese, ricotta, Parmesan, mayonnaise, Italian seasoning, salt, and pepper in a large bowl. Stir in spinach and artichoke hearts. Set aside.

MAKE THE PARMESAN BÉCHAMEL SAUCE: Melt the butter with the red pepper flakes in a skillet over medium heat. Whisk in the flour and cook, stirring constantly, for 1 minute. Gradually whisk in the milk. Cook, whisking frequently, until the mixture thickens. Stir in the Parmesan cheese.

ASSEMBLE: Spread 1 cup of the béchamel sauce in the bottom of the prepared dish. Top with 3 noodles, breaking some to fit the pan. Spread about one-third of the spinach-artichoke filling over the noodles and top with one-third of the remaining sauce. Repeat 2 more times in this order: noodles, spinach-artichoke filling, and sauce. Sprinkle the lasagna with the mozzarella cheese.

COVER AND BAKE for 30 minutes. Uncover and bake for 10 minutes until golden brown. Let stand for 10 minutes before serving.

VEGETARIAN

Simple Spinach & Ricotta Roll Ups

This is one of the easiest lasagnas in this book! You can keep the ingredients in the pantry, fridge, or freezer for months, making this a fantastic last-minute dinner option. To keep it vegetarian but boost the protein, stir some thawed vegetarian meat crumbles into the pasta sauce and proceed.

~~~~~~~~~~~~~~~~~~ **SERVES 4** ~~~~~~~~~~~~~~~~~~

8 lasagna noodles

SPINACH-RICOTTA FILLING
1 (15-ounce) container ricotta cheese

1 (9-ounce) box frozen spinach, thawed and squeezed dry

1 large egg

1 teaspoon Italian seasoning

½ teaspoon garlic powder

¼ teaspoon fine sea salt

1 (24-ounce) jar pasta or marinara sauce

1 cup (4 ounces) shredded mozzarella cheese

PREHEAT THE OVEN to 350°F. Lightly grease a 13 x 9-inch baking dish.

COOK THE LASAGNA NOODLES in salted boiling water according to the package directions. Drain, then rinse with cool water.

MAKE THE SPINACH-RICOTTA FILLING: Stir together the ricotta, spinach, egg, Italian seasoning, garlic powder, and salt in a large bowl.

ASSEMBLE: Pour half of the pasta sauce in the bottom of the prepared baking dish. Place the noodles in batches on a work surface. Spread the ricotta cheese filling evenly along the lasagna noodle and roll it up into a spiral. Place the rolled pasta, seam side down, on the sauce. Drizzle the remaining sauce over the roll ups and sprinkle with the mozzarella.

COVER AND BAKE for 30 minutes. Uncover and bake for 15 minutes until golden brown. Let stand for 10 minutes before serving.

Creamed Spinach
& Mushroom Lasagna

Mascarpone is a super-rich double- or triple-cream cheese that has a very mild flavor. You can substitute Neufchâtel or cream cheese. The spinach mixture might release liquid, and that's okay since the oven-ready noodles need moisture to expand and cook. If you use traditional boiled lasagna noodles, you can sprinkle about a quarter cup of breadcrumbs in the bottom of the dish to absorb any excess liquid.

~~~~~~~~~~~~~ **SERVES 4** ~~~~~~~~~~~~~

CREAMED SPINACH

- **2 tablespoons extra-virgin olive oil**
- **1 shallot, minced**
- **1 (8- to 10-ounce) container sliced mushrooms**
- **½ cup white wine**
- **½ teaspoon fine sea salt**
- **½ teaspoon freshly ground black pepper**
- **1 (16-ounce) container or 2 (10-ounce) containers fresh baby spinach**
- **1 (8-ounce) container mascarpone cheese**
- **½ cup (2 ounces) shredded Parmesan cheese**

RICOTTA FILLING

- **1 (15-ounce) container ricotta or cottage cheese**
- **3 tablespoons prepared pesto sauce**
- **2 large eggs**
- **½ teaspoon fine sea salt**
- **⅛ teaspoon freshly ground black pepper**

- **9 oven-ready lasagna noodles**
- **½ cup (2 ounces) shredded or grated Parmesan cheese**

PREHEAT THE OVEN to 350°F. Lightly grease a 12 x 7-inch or 9 x 9-inch baking dish.

MAKE THE CREAMED SPINACH: Heat the oil in a large skillet over medium-high. Add the shallot, mushrooms, wine, salt, and pepper. Cook, stirring frequently, for 7 to 9 minutes or until the mushrooms are tender. Add the spinach in batches and cook, tossing occasionally with tongs, for 5 minutes or until the spinach wilts. Stir in the mascarpone and Parmesan.

MAKE THE RICOTTA FILLING: Combine the ricotta, pesto, eggs, salt, and pepper in a bowl.

ASSEMBLE: Spoon about 1 cup of the spinach mixture in the bottom of the prepared baking dish. Top with 3 noodles, breaking to fit the pan, if necessary. Top with one-third of the ricotta filling and one-third of the remaining spinach mixture. Repeat twice with remaining noodles, ricotta filling, and spinach mixture. Sprinkle the top with the Parmesan cheese.

COVER AND BAKE for 50 minutes or until the noodles are tender. Let stand for 10 minutes before serving.

Deep-Dish Lasagna Puttanesca

Kalamata olives and capers are essential ingredients in Puttanesca sauce. They are naturally very salty, so sample a spoonful of the sauce before adding a quarter teaspoon of salt, if you think it's necessary. Although the anchovies are optional to keep this a vegetarian option, they add a briny, savory flavor, too.

~~~~~~~~ **SERVES 8** ~~~~~~~~

12 to 16 lasagna noodles

PUTTANESCA SAUCE

2 tablespoons extra-virgin olive oil

1 onion, chopped

¼ teaspoon chili pepper flakes

1 eggplant, peeled and coarsely chopped

2 zucchini, coarsely chopped

3 large garlic cloves, minced

½ teaspoon freshly ground black pepper

½ to 1 teaspoon anchovy paste (optional)

½ cup kalamata olives, sliced

1 tablespoon capers, drained

2 (28-ounce) cans fire-roasted crushed or diced tomatoes, undrained

1 teaspoon sugar

2 tablespoons chopped fresh basil

RICOTTA FILLING

1 (15-ounce) container ricotta cheese

1 large egg

¼ teaspoon fine sea salt

¼ teaspoon freshly ground black pepper

1 cup (4 ounces) grated or shredded Parmesan cheese

8 ounces fresh mozzarella, sliced, or 2 cups shredded mozzarella

PREHEAT THE OVEN to 375°F. Lightly grease a 13 x 9-inch deep baking dish.

COOK THE LASAGNA NOODLES in boiling salted water according to the package directions. Drain, then rinse in cool water. Cover with plastic wrap until ready to use.

MAKE THE PUTTANESCA SAUCE: Heat the oil in a large skillet over medium-high. Add the onion and pepper flakes; cook for 3 minutes until tender. Add the eggplant and zucchini and cook, stirring frequently, for 5 to 7 minutes until tender. Add the garlic and pepper and cook, stirring frequently, for 2 minutes. Stir in the anchovy paste, if using, the olives, capers, tomatoes, and sugar. Simmer over medium-low heat, stirring frequently, for 20 minutes. Stir in the fresh basil.

MAKE THE RICOTTA FILLING: Combine the ricotta, egg, salt, and pepper in a medium bowl.

ASSEMBLE: Spread one-third of the Puttanesca sauce over the bottom of the prepared dish. Layer the ingredients in this order: 3 to 4 noodles, half of the ricotta filling, 3 or 4 noodles, one-third of the sauce, 3 or 4 noodles, remaining ricotta, 3 or 4 noodles, and remaining sauce. Top evenly with the Parmesan cheese.

COVER AND BAKE for 35 to 40 minutes. Uncover and place the fresh mozzarella slices over the top. Bake for another 10 minutes until the cheese melts. Let stand for 10 minutes before serving.

VEGETARIAN

Paneer Masala Gluten-Free Lasagna

Often used in Indian dishes, Paneer cheese is a simple, unripened cheese that's been pressed to a firm texture. Its mild flavor is similar to Mexican queso fresco. You can substitute a large-curd cottage cheese that's been drained well. For a stronger flavored substitution, cut an eight-ounce block of feta cheese into cubes.

SERVES 8

MASALA BUTTER SAUCE

3 tablespoons ghee or butter

1 small onion, finely chopped

2 garlic cloves, minced

2 teaspoons minced fresh ginger

2 teaspoons garam masala

1 teaspoon ground turmeric

1 tablespoon chili powder

¾ teaspoon fine sea salt

¼ teaspoon freshly ground black pepper

1 (28-ounce) can crushed tomatoes

1 (15-ounce) can chickpeas, rinsed and drained

½ teaspoon sugar

¾ cup heavy cream

SPINACH-CARDAMOM BÉCHAMEL SAUCE

2 tablespoons butter

3 tablespoons brown rice flour or gluten-free flour mix

¼ teaspoon ground coriander

¼ teaspoon ground cardamom

¼ teaspoon fine sea salt

⅛ teaspoon ground white pepper

2 cups half and half

2 (11-ounce) packages fresh spinach leaves

1 (12-ounce) package paneer cheese, cut into small cubes

1 (9-ounce) package oven-ready brown rice or green lentil lasagna noodles

1 cup (4 ounces) shredded Parmesan cheese

PREHEAT THE OVEN to 350°F. Lightly grease a 13 x 9-inch baking dish.

MAKE THE MASALA BUTTER SAUCE: Melt the butter in a large skillet over medium heat. Add the onion, garlic, and ginger and cook, stirring occasionally, for 5 to 7 minutes or until tender. Stir in the garam masala, turmeric, chili powder, salt, and pepper. Add the tomatoes, chickpeas, and sugar and cook, stirring occasionally, for 20 minutes or until the sauce is thickened. Stir in the cream. Transfer to a bowl.

MAKE THE SPINACH-CARDAMOM BÉCHAMEL SAUCE: Melt the butter in a large skillet over medium-high heat. Whisk in the rice flour, coriander, cardamom, salt, and white pepper. Cook, stirring constantly, for 1 minute. Whisk in the half and half and spinach and cook, stirring frequently, for 5 minutes or until thickened and the spinach is wilted. Remove from the heat and stir in the paneer.

ASSEMBLE: Spread ½ cup of the butter sauce in the bottom of the prepared dish and top with 4 noodles, breaking some of the noodles to fit the pan. Top with one-third of the remaining butter sauce and one-third of the béchamel sauce. Repeat twice with 4 noodles, one-third butter sauce, and one-third béchamel sauce. Sprinkle the top with the Parmesan cheese.

COVER AND BAKE for 40 minutes. Uncover and bake for 10 minutes until golden brown. Let stand for 10 minutes before serving.

VEGETARIAN

Tossed Lasagna with Pesto & Roma Tomatoes

A bit of fresh lemon keeps the bright green color in pesto. For a twist, substitute arugula for the basil and walnuts or almonds for the pine nuts. Toasting the nuts enhances the texture and flavor. I usually toast large quantities in the oven, then freeze them in freezer bags for up to three months, until I need to add a bit of crunch to salads, sandwiches, or cheese appetizers.

~~~~~~~~~~ **SERVES 8** ~~~~~~~~~~

PESTO SAUCE

1 (4-ounce) container fresh basil

1 garlic clove

½ cup (2 ounces) shredded or grated Parmesan cheese

½ cup extra-virgin olive oil

½ teaspoon lemon zest

1 tablespoon lemon juice

¼ teaspoon fine sea salt

¼ cup toasted pine nuts

12 lasagna noodles

RICOTTA FILLING

1 (15-ounce) container ricotta cheese

1 large egg

¼ teaspoon fine sea salt

¼ teaspoon freshly ground black pepper

3 to 4 Roma tomatoes, sliced ⅛ inch thick and seeded

⅔ cup seasoned panko breadcrumbs

⅓ cup shredded or grated Parmesan cheese

¼ teaspoon freshly ground black pepper

2 tablespoons butter, melted

4 ounces fresh mozzarella cheese, chopped

PREHEAT THE OVEN to 350°F. Lightly grease a 13 x 9-inch baking dish.

MAKE THE PESTO SAUCE: Combine the basil, garlic, Parmesan, olive oil, lemon zest and juice, and salt in a food processor; pulse until finely chopped. Add the pine nuts and pulse until finely chopped. Transfer to a large bowl.

COOK THE LASAGNA NOODLES in boiling salted water according to the package directions. Drain well, and add the warm noodles to the pesto, tossing well.

MAKE THE RICOTTA FILLING: Combine the ricotta, egg, salt, and pepper in a medium bowl.

ASSEMBLE: Place a layer of 4 noodles in the bottom of the prepared dish. Top with one-third of the ricotta mixture. Repeat two more times with 4 noodles and one-third of the ricotta mixture. Arrange the tomato slices on top of the lasagna.

STIR TOGETHER the panko, Parmesan, pepper, and melted butter in a medium bowl. Sprinkle the mixture evenly over the tomatoes.

COVER AND BAKE for 30 minutes. Uncover and arrange the fresh mozzarella on the top of the lasagna. Bake for 10 more minutes or until the mozzarella melts. Let stand for 10 minutes before serving.

Roasted Eggplant & Hummus Lasagna

Baba ghanoush is an eggplant dip that is similar to hummus except it includes eggplant instead of chickpeas. This recipe steals some of those flavors, using the eggplant as the "noodle" to make it gluten-free and keto-friendly. Use whatever flavor of prepared hummus you prefer— garlic, lemon, or roasted red bell pepper are all good choices.

SERVES 4

1 large eggplant

½ teaspoon fine sea salt

2 tablespoons extra-virgin olive oil

MEATLESS "MEAT" SAUCE

1 tablespoon extra-virgin olive oil

½ onion, chopped

1 garlic clove, minced

1 (12-ounce) package frozen meatless crumbles, thawed

2 tablespoons chopped fresh or 2 teaspoons dried mint

1 tablespoon chopped fresh or 1 teaspoon dried oregano

¼ teaspoon ground allspice

1 cup pasta or marinara sauce

TOFU-HUMMUS FILLING

1 (14-ounce) container tofu

1 (8-ounce) container garlic-flavored hummus

¼ teaspoon fine sea salt

1 cup (4 ounces) shredded Parmesan cheese

PREHEAT THE OVEN to 425°F. Lightly grease an 8 x 8-inch baking dish. Place a wire cooling rack over a baking sheet.

PEEL THE EGGPLANT and slice lengthwise ⅛ to ¼ inch thick. Sprinkle the salt evenly over both sides. Place on a wire rack and let stand for 10 to 20 minutes. Blot dry with paper towels. Brush both sides evenly with the olive oil. Bake on the rack for 10 minutes on each side until tender and browned along the edges. Reduce the heat to 375°F.

MAKE THE MEATLESS "MEAT" SAUCE: Heat the olive oil in a large nonstick skillet over medium. Add the onion and garlic and cook, stirring occasionally for 2 minutes. Stir in the meatless crumbles, mint, oregano, and allspice. Stir in the pasta sauce and cook, stirring occasionally, for 5 minutes.

MAKE THE TOFU-HUMMUS FILLING: Mash together the tofu, hummus, and salt in a small bowl. Set aside.

ASSEMBLE: Spread 1 cup of the meatless sauce in the bottom of the prepared dish. Arrange half of the eggplant over the sauce, spread with half of the tofu mixture, and sprinkle with half of the Parmesan cheese. Repeat with the remaining eggplant, sauce, tofu mixture, and cheese.

COVER AND BAKE for 30 minutes. Uncover and bake for another 10 minutes until golden brown. Let stand for 10 minutes before serving.

VEGETARIAN

Eggplant & Lentil Lasagna

Red lentils don't hold their shape when cooked but create
a rich, thickly textured sauce when mixed with marinara.
You can create the sauce with any bean you prefer as long
as they are cooked through before assembling the dish.

~~~~~~~~~~ SERVES 8 ~~~~~~~~~~

2 eggplants

1 teaspoon fine sea salt

3 tablespoons extra-virgin
olive oil

RED LENTIL SAUCE

1 tablespoon extra-virgin
olive oil

1 small onion, finely chopped

1 red bell pepper, finely
chopped

2 garlic cloves, finely chopped

2 small celery stalks, finely
chopped

2 carrots, finely chopped

1 cup uncooked red lentils

1½ cups vegetable broth

1 (24-ounce) jar pasta or
marinara sauce

CILANTRO BÉCHAMEL SAUCE

2 tablespoons butter

2 tablespoons all-purpose flour

2½ cups half and half or
whole milk

½ teaspoon fine sea salt

½ teaspoon ground cumin

½ cup (2 ounces) shredded
or grated Parmesan cheese

½ cup lightly packed fresh
cilantro, chopped

8 oven-ready lasagna noodles

1 cup (4 ounces) shredded
mozzarella cheese

PREHEAT THE OVEN to
425°F. Lightly grease a
13 x 9-inch baking dish.
Place a wire cooling rack
over a baking sheet.

PEEL THE EGGPLANT and
slice lengthwise ⅛ to ¼ inch
thick. Sprinkle the salt evenly
over both sides. Place on the
wire rack and let stand for
10 to 20 minutes. Blot dry
with paper towels. Brush
both sides evenly with the
olive oil. Bake on the rack for
10 minutes on each side until
tender and browned along
the edges. Remove and reduce
the temperature to 350°F.

**MAKE THE RED LENTIL
SAUCE:** Heat the oil in a
saucepan over medium heat.
Add the onion and bell pepper
and cook, stirring occasionally,
for 5 minutes. Add the garlic,
celery, and carrots and cook,
stirring occasionally, for
5 minutes. Stir in the lentils,
broth, and pasta sauce. Bring
the mixture to a boil. Cover,
reduce the heat to low, and
simmer for 15 minutes or until
the mixture thickens and the
lentils are tender.

**MAKE THE CILANTRO
BÉCHAMEL SAUCE:** Melt the
butter in a large skillet over
medium-high heat. Whisk in
the flour and cook, stirring
constantly, for 1 minute. Whisk
in the half and half, salt, and
cumin. Cook, stirring frequently,
for 5 minutes or until the mixture
thickens. Add the Parmesan and
cook, stirring occasionally, until
the sauce is smooth. Stir in the
cilantro.

ASSEMBLE: Spread ½ cup
of the béchamel sauce in the
bottom of the prepared baking
dish. Top with 4 noodles,
breaking to fit the dish. Top
the noodles with one-half of
the lentil sauce, one-half of the
eggplant, and one-half of the
remaining béchamel sauce.
Repeat in this order: noodles,
lentil, eggplant, and béchamel
sauce. Sprinkle with the
mozzarella cheese.

COVER AND BAKE for
30 minutes. Uncover and bake
for 15 minutes more until golden
brown. Let stand for 10 minutes
before serving.

Creamy Tomato & Three-Onion Lasagna

For vegetarians craving the rich flavor of Bolognese, try this sauce that uses frozen meat crumbles. The faux ground beef often tastes very plain, so I added a variety of onions. They slightly caramelize, giving the sauce a naturally sweet taste. To give the sauce creaminess, I used half and half, and more of it than usual in a Bolognese. The extra dairy balances the acidity of the fresh tomatoes.

SERVES 8

8 lasagna noodles

THREE-ONION "BOLOGNESE" SAUCE

1 tablespoon butter

2 tablespoons extra-virgin olive oil

3 to 4 leeks, washed well and chopped

1 small yellow onion, chopped

1 small red onion, chopped

¼ teaspoon crushed red pepper flakes

2 tablespoons white wine

2 garlic cloves, minced

1 pound small round or Roma tomatoes, coarsely chopped

1 teaspoon Italian seasoning

½ teaspoon fine sea salt

1 (12- to 16-ounce) package frozen meatless beef crumbles, thawed

1½ cups half and half

1 cup (4 ounces) shredded Gouda, provolone, or Italian blend cheese

½ cup (2 ounces) shredded or grated Parmesan cheese

PREHEAT THE OVEN to 350°F. Lightly grease a 13 x 9-inch baking dish.

COOK THE LASAGNA NOODLES in salted boiling water according to the package directions. Drain, then rinse in cool water.

MAKE THE THREE-ONION "BOLOGNESE" SAUCE: Melt the butter with the oil in a large skillet over medium-high heat. Add the leeks, yellow onion, red onion, and red pepper flakes. Cook, stirring frequently, for 5 minutes or until tender. Add the wine and cook for 1 minute or until it evaporates. Add the garlic, tomatoes, Italian seasoning, and salt. Cook, stirring frequently, for 5 minutes or until the tomatoes are tender. Add the meatless crumbles and cook, stirring frequently, for 2 minutes or until the mixture is hot. Stir in the half and half and cook, stirring occasionally, for 3 to 5 minutes or until slightly thickened.

ASSEMBLE: Spread ½ cup of the sauce in the bottom of the prepared baking dish. Top with 4 noodles, cutting and layering to fit the pan. Spread half of the sauce over the noodles and sprinkle with half of the cheese. Repeat with remaining noodles, sauce, and cheese. Sprinkle with Parmesan cheese.

COVER AND BAKE for 30 minutes or until hot and bubbly. Uncover and bake 10 minutes more or until golden brown. Let stand for 10 minutes before serving.

VEGETARIAN

Zucchini Planks & Cheese Lasagna

Anyone with a backyard garden understands the need for as many zucchini recipes as you can think to create. I am always looking for a new way to prepare squash, and this easy one is both gluten-free and keto-friendly. When there's no starchy noodles to absorb moisture, the lasagna should be layered with cooked zucchini, since raw zucchini might release too much liquid during cooking. You can even grill the planks to add a richer, smoky flavor.

~~~~~~~~~~~~~~~~~~ **SERVES 6** ~~~~~~~~~~~~~~~~~~

4 zucchini

1 teaspoon fine sea salt

RICOTTA FILLING

1 (15-ounce) container ricotta cheese

2 cups (8 ounces) shredded mozzarella cheese

1 cup (4 ounces) shredded Parmesan cheese

1 large egg

¼ teaspoon freshly ground black pepper

2 cups pasta or marinara sauce

Chopped fresh basil

PREHEAT THE OVEN to 375°F. Lightly grease a 13 x 9-inch baking dish. Line two sheet pans with parchment paper.

CUT THE ENDS FROM THE ZUCCHINI and slice thinly (⅛ to ¼ inch thick) with a mandoline slicer or sharp knife. Sprinkle each side with salt and place in a single layer on the prepared baking sheets. Let stand for 15 minutes. Blot each side with paper towels to remove excess moisture. Bake the zucchini for 10 minutes.

MAKE THE RICOTTA FILLING: Combine the ricotta, mozzarella, Parmesan, egg, and pepper in a medium bowl.

ASSEMBLE: Spread about ½ cup of the pasta sauce in the bottom of the prepared dish. Arrange one-third of the zucchini slices over the sauce. Top with one-third of the ricotta filling. Repeat twice in this order: sauce, zucchini, and ricotta.

BAKE, UNCOVERED, for 40 minutes until hot and bubbly. Let stand for 10 minutes before serving. Sprinkle with the chopped basil.

Veggie Lasagna Pockets

These flavorful packages are a clever and pretty way to prepare individual lasagna servings. Since the noodles are not immersed in sauce, it's important to keep the dish covered while baking so the pasta doesn't dry out. I use oven-ready noodles because they are a bit wider and become more pliable with a quick soak in warm water than traditional lasagna noodles.

SERVES 6

ZUCCHINI, KALE &
SUN-DRIED TOMATO FILLING

- 1 tablespoon extra-virgin olive oil
- ¼ onion, finely chopped
- ⅛ teaspoon crushed red pepper flakes
- ¼ teaspoon fine sea salt
- ½ teaspoon freshly ground black pepper
- 1 garlic clove, minced
- 1 zucchini, finely chopped
- 1 cup chopped fresh kale, collards, or spinach
- ½ cup packed sun-dried tomatoes, chopped

BÉCHAMEL SAUCE

- 2 tablespoons butter
- 2½ tablespoons all-purpose flour
- 1½ cups half and half or whole milk
- ¼ teaspoon ground nutmeg
- ¼ teaspoon fine sea salt

- 12 oven-ready lasagna noodles
- ¾ cup (3 ounces) shredded Parmesan cheese
- ¼ cup mixed chopped fresh herbs, such as basil, parsley, or rosemary

PREHEAT THE OVEN to 375°F. Lightly grease a 13 x 9-inch baking dish.

MAKE THE ZUCCHINI, KALE, AND SUN-DRIED TOMATO FILLING: Heat the olive oil in a large skillet over medium-high. Add the onion, red pepper flakes, salt, and pepper. Cook for 5 minutes or until the onion is tender. Stir in the garlic and zucchini and cook, stirring frequently, for 5 minutes or until the vegetables are tender. Stir in the kale and sun-dried tomatoes. Cook, stirring occasionally, for 3 minutes or until the kale wilts. Transfer the vegetable mixture to a bowl to use the same skillet, if desired.

MAKE THE BÉCHAMEL SAUCE: Melt the butter in a large skillet over medium heat. Whisk in the flour and cook, stirring constantly, for 1 minute. Whisk in the half and half, nutmeg, and salt. Cook, stirring frequently, for 5 minutes or until the mixture thickens.

SOAK THE LASAGNA NOODLES in warm water for about 30 minutes or until pliable.

ASSEMBLE: Spoon half of the béchamel sauce in the bottom of the prepared dish. Place a lasagna noodle horizontally on a work surface. Place another noodle across the first vertically so the two noodles form a plus sign. Spoon about ¼ cup of the vegetable mixture in the center. Top with 1 tablespoon of the Parmesan cheese. Fold the flaps up to form a packet. Carefully turn over and place on the béchamel sauce in the prepared baking dish. Repeat with the remaining noodles, vegetable mixture, and Parmesan cheese. Spoon the remaining béchamel sauce over the packets and top each one evenly with the remaining Parmesan cheese.

COVER AND BAKE for 30 minutes. Uncover and bake for 20 minutes or until golden brown. Let stand for 10 minutes before serving. Sprinkle the tops evenly with chopped fresh herbs.

Wild Mushroom & Three-Cheese Lasagna

I use the term "wild mushroom" pretty loosely since I don't really expect people to forage for their dinner, and saying "edible mushrooms" is pretty off-putting! In this case, "wild" means anything other than the common button mushroom (although you can substitute those if you wish).

～ SERVES 8 ～

9 lasagna noodles

WILD MUSHROOM SAUCE

4 tablespoons butter

1 pound portobello, cremini, or mixed wild mushrooms, sliced

1 onion, chopped

3 garlic cloves, finely chopped

2 teaspoons fresh thyme leaves

½ teaspoon fine sea salt

½ teaspoon freshly ground black pepper

¼ cup all-purpose flour

2 tablespoons sherry or white wine

2½ cups half and half or whole milk

½ teaspoon ground nutmeg

1 cup (4 ounces) shredded mozzarella cheese

1 cup (4 ounces) shredded Havarti cheese

½ cup (2 ounces) shredded or grated Parmesan cheese

2 tablespoons mixed chopped fresh herbs such as parsley, thyme, or oregano

PREHEAT OVEN to 375°F. Lightly grease a 13 x 9-inch baking dish.

COOK THE NOODLES in boiling salted water according to the package directions. Drain, then rinse in cool water.

MAKE THE WILD MUSHROOM SAUCE: Melt the butter in a large skillet over medium-high heat. Add the mushrooms, onions, garlic, thyme, salt, and pepper. Cook, stirring frequently, for 5 to 8 minutes or until the mushrooms are tender and most of the liquid evaporates. Add the flour and cook, stirring constantly, for 1 minute. Stir in the sherry and cook, stirring frequently, for 2 minutes or until it evaporates. Slowly stir in the half and half and nutmeg. Cook over medium heat for 5 to 7 minutes or until the mixture thickens.

COMBINE THE MOZZARELLA, Havarti, and Parmesan in a bowl, tossing until well blended.

ASSEMBLE: Spread one cup of the mushroom sauce in the bottom of the prepared baking dish. Top with a layer of 3 noodles, 1 cup mushroom sauce, and sprinkle with ¾ cup of the cheese mixture. Repeat 2 more times, layering the noodles, mushroom sauce, and cheese.

COVER WITH FOIL and bake for 30 minutes. Uncover and bake an additional 20 minutes or until golden brown. Let stand for 10 minutes, then sprinkle with the chopped herbs before serving.

101 LASAGNAS & OTHER LAYERED CASSEROLES

Portobello "Bacon" & Tomato Lasagna

The texture of packaged faux bacon can get a bit "squeaky" between your teeth, but meaty, tender mushrooms make a great substitution when marinated in liquid smoke, sweet maple, and salty soy sauce. I recommend portobello mushrooms because they are large and more closely resemble slices of bacon when sliced. If preferred, use sliced cremini or other round, meaty mushrooms. Be sure to remove the tomato seeds and gel before assembling; otherwise, the lasagna may get watery on the bottom.

SERVES 4 TO 6

PORTOBELLO "BACON"

¼ cup extra-virgin olive oil

2 tablespoons maple syrup

2 tablespoons soy sauce

2 teaspoons hot sauce

1 teaspoon liquid smoke

½ teaspoon fine sea salt

¼ teaspoon garlic powder

1 pound portobello mushrooms

SEASONED TOMATOES

4 medium or 6 Roma tomatoes, thinly sliced and seeded

1 small red onion, quartered and sliced

¼ cup chopped fresh basil

2 tablespoons extra-virgin olive oil

⅛ teaspoon crushed red pepper flakes

½ teaspoon fine sea salt

¼ teaspoon freshly ground black pepper

4 oven-ready lasagna noodles

½ (5-ounce) container baby arugula

2 tablespoons butter, melted

½ cup panko breadcrumbs

½ cup (2 ounces) shredded Parmesan cheese

PREHEAT THE OVEN to 375°F. Line two rimmed sheet pans with nonstick foil. Lightly grease an 8 x 8-inch baking dish.

MAKE THE PORTOBELLO "BACON": Combine the olive oil, maple syrup, soy sauce, hot sauce, liquid smoke, salt, and garlic powder in a large bowl. Slice the mushrooms ⅛ inch thick. Add the mushrooms to the bowl, tossing until well coated. Spread in a single layer on the prepared sheet pans. Bake for 30 minutes, rotating the pans after 15 minutes, until the mushrooms are tender and dry, and any liquid has evaporated.

MAKE THE SEASONED TOMATOES: Combine the tomatoes, onion, basil, oil, red pepper flakes, salt, and pepper in a large bowl.

ASSEMBLE: Spoon one-third of the tomato mixture into the bottom of the prepared baking dish. Top with two noodles, breaking them to fit the pan. Spread half the portobello "bacon," half the arugula, and one-third of the tomato mixture over the noodles. Repeat with the remaining noodles, portobello "bacon," arugula, and one-third of the tomato mixture.

COMBINE THE BUTTER, breadcrumbs, and Parmesan in a bowl. Sprinkle over the lasagna. Cover and bake for 25 minutes. Uncover and bake for 15 minutes or until golden brown. Let stand for 10 minutes before serving.

VEGETARIAN

Soy Chorizo & Black Beans with Polenta

This dish has it all—great flavor, low cost, simple to prepare, and looks pretty. Plus, you can keep most of the ingredients in the refrigerator or pantry for weeks, making it a dinner you can whip up at the spur of the moment. Carnivores can replace the soy chorizo with traditional fresh Mexican chorizo for a similar flavor. Spanish and Portuguese chorizo is cured and smoked with a firm texture like salami. You can use that, too, but the mixture only needs to be heated since it's already cooked.

~~~~~~~~~~~ **SERVES 6** ~~~~~~~~~~~

POLENTA

4 cups vegetable broth

½ teaspoon fine sea salt

1¼ cups quick-cooking polenta or grits

2 tablespoons butter

½ cup (4 ounces) shredded cheddar cheese

SOY CHORIZO FILLING

1 tablespoon extra-virgin olive oil

½ onion, chopped

2 garlic cloves, minced

1 (12-ounce) package soy chorizo, crumbled

1 (14-ounce) can diced fire-roasted tomatoes, undrained

1 (14-ounce) can black beans, rinsed and drained

1 (9- or 12-ounce) package frozen spinach, thawed and squeezed dry

1 cup (4 ounces) shredded Monterey Jack, Mexican cheese blend, or mozzarella cheese

1 cup (4 ounces) shredded Parmesan cheese

Chopped fresh cilantro

PREHEAT THE OVEN to 350°F. Lightly grease a 6-cup or 8 x 8-inch baking dish.

MAKE THE POLENTA: Bring the broth and salt to a boil in a large saucepan over medium-high heat. Whisk in the polenta, cover, and cook, stirring occasionally, for 5 to 7 minutes or until the polenta is tender. Add the butter, stirring until the butter melts and the mixture is well blended. Stir in the cheddar cheese. Keep covered.

MAKE THE SOY CHORIZO FILLING: Heat the oil in a large skillet over medium-high. Add the onion, garlic, and soy chorizo. Cook, stirring constantly, for 5 minutes or until the onion is tender and the mixture is crumbly. Stir in the tomatoes and cook, stirring constantly, for 10 minutes until the mixture thickens. Stir in the black beans (save a few black beans to garnish, if desired).

ASSEMBLE: Spoon half of the polenta mixture in the bottom of prepared dish and top with the chorizo filling and spinach. Cover with the remaining polenta mixture and garnish the top with some of the reserved black beans, if desired. Sprinkle the top with the Monterey Jack and Parmesan cheese.

COVER AND BAKE for 30 minutes. Uncover and broil for 3 minutes or until golden brown and bubbly. Let stand for 10 minutes before serving. Sprinkle with the cilantro.

Kale, Roasted Bell Pepper & Goat Cheese Lasagna

If you shortcut this recipe by purchasing pre-chopped kale in a bag, make sure to thoroughly dry the leaves. The bagged type is usually curly kale, and moisture will remain in all the nooks unless patted dry. For a change of pace, try crumbled feta cheese instead of the goat cheese. Adding red pepper flakes, fresh thyme, and sautéed onions and garlic helps give the jarred pasta sauce a fresher taste.

SERVES 4

8 cups chopped fresh kale

RICOTTA–GOAT CHEESE FILLING

1 (15-ounce) container ricotta cheese

5 to 6 ounces soft goat cheese

1 large egg

¼ teaspoon fine sea salt

¼ teaspoon freshly ground black pepper

PUMPED-UP PASTA SAUCE

1 tablespoon extra-virgin olive oil

¼ onion, minced

2 garlic cloves, minced

1 teaspoon fresh thyme leaves

¼ teaspoon red pepper flakes

1 (24-ounce) jar pasta or marinara sauce

1 tablespoon red wine

5 to 6 gluten-free, oven-ready lasagna noodles

2 roasted red bell peppers, fresh roasted or jarred, sliced or chopped

½ cup (2 ounces) shredded Parmesan cheese

PREHEAT THE OVEN to 350°F. Lightly grease an 8 x 8-inch baking dish.

COOK THE KALE in boiling salted water to cover for 3 to 5 minutes until tender. Drain in a colander, then rinse with cool water. Press the kale to remove excess water. Let dry on paper towels.

MAKE THE RICOTTA–GOAT CHEESE FILLING: Combine the ricotta and goat cheese in a small bowl, mashing until well blended. Stir in the egg, salt, and pepper.

MAKE THE PUMPED-UP PASTA SAUCE: Heat the oil in a skillet over medium heat. Add the onion, garlic, thyme, and red pepper flakes. Cook, stirring frequently, for 3 to 5 minutes or until the onion is tender. Stir in the pasta sauce and red wine. Cook, stirring occasionally, for 5 minutes or until thickened.

ASSEMBLE: Spread ¾ cup of the pasta sauce in the bottom of the prepared dish. Top with 2 to 2½ lasagna noodles, breaking to fit pan. Top the noodles with half of the ricotta filling. Spread half of the chopped kale over the ricotta and sprinkle with half of the bell pepper. Top with half of the remaining sauce. Repeat in this order: noodles, ricotta filling, kale mixture, remaining bell pepper, noodles, and sauce. Sprinkle with the Parmesan over the top.

COVER AND BAKE for 30 minutes. Uncover and bake for 15 minutes more until golden brown and bubbly. Let stand for 10 minutes before serving.

Vegetable Crepe Lasagna

A vintage Julia Child recipe was the inspiration for this adaptation that, even with the long length, takes a few shortcuts. The flavors aren't complicated, and the simple seasonings enhance each vegetable. After you make it the first time (be prepared for future requests), you can multitask the veggies, shaving time off the prep. Expect a lot of oohs and aahs at potlucks, and houseguests will swoon if you serve this for brunch. You can make your own crepes, but the refrigerated packaged ones are easy, and each one is exactly the right size.

~~~~~~~~~~ **SERVES 8 TO 10** ~~~~~~~~~~

MUSHROOM FILLING

- 2 (8-ounce) packages cremini or button mushrooms
- 1 shallot, coarsely chopped
- 2 tablespoons butter
- 2 teaspoons red wine
- ¼ teaspoon fine sea salt
- ¼ teaspoon freshly ground black pepper

CARROT FILLING

- 2 tablespoons butter
- 1 pound carrots or baby carrots, julienne cut (matchsticks)
- ¼ teaspoon fine sea salt
- ¼ teaspoon freshly ground black pepper
- 1 teaspoon chopped fresh dill

BROCCOLI FILLING

- 6 cups fresh or frozen and thawed broccoli florets
- ¼ teaspoon fine sea salt
- ¼ teaspoon freshly ground black pepper

CREAM CHEESE CUSTARD

- 6 large eggs
- 1 (8-ounce) package cream cheese, softened
- 1 cup heavy cream or half and half

- ⅛ teaspoon ground nutmeg
- ⅛ teaspoon cayenne pepper

- 1 (5-ounce) package refrigerated prepared crepes or 10 (9-inch) crepes
- 2 cups (8 ounces) shredded Swiss cheese

MAKE THE MUSHROOM FILLING: Place the mushrooms and shallot in a food processor. Pulse several times until finely chopped. Melt the butter in a large skillet over medium heat. Add the mushroom mixture, wine, salt, and pepper. Cook, stirring occasionally, for 20 minutes or until the liquid evaporates.

MAKE THE CARROT FILLING: Melt the butter in a large skillet over medium heat. Add the carrots, ¼ cup water, the salt, and pepper. Cover and cook, stirring frequently, for 7 to 10 minutes or until the carrots are tender. Stir in the dill.

MAKE THE BROCCOLI FILLING: Cook the broccoli in boiling salted water cover for 5 minutes or until tender. Drain in a colander, then rinse with cold water. Coarsely chop and transfer to a medium bowl. Stir in the salt and pepper.

MAKE THE CUSTARD: Combine the eggs, cream cheese, heavy cream, nutmeg, and cayenne in a food processor. Process until smooth and well blended.

ASSEMBLE: Preheat the oven to 350°F. Line a 9-inch springform or 3-inch-deep cake pan with buttered foil or parchment paper.

LAYER ABOUT 4 TO 5 CREPES around the sides of the prepared pan, allowing them to overlap in the center to cover the bottom (about one-third of the crepes will hang over the sides). Spread one-third of the Swiss cheese over the crepes. Press all of the carrots over the cheese. Pour 1¼ cups of the custard over the carrots. Arrange 1 crepe over the custard. Sprinkle the top of the crepe with one-third of the cheese. Spread all of the mushroom filling over the cheese. Drizzle with 1¼ cups custard. Arrange 1 crepe over the custard. Sprinkle the top of the crepe with the remaining cheese. Top with the broccoli filling and drizzle with the remaining custard. Top with a crepe and fold the overlapping edges of the crepe over the top.

COVER WITH FOIL and place on a baking sheet to catch any drips. Bake for 1 to 1½ hours. Check the temperature in the center of the pan at 1 hour. Continue to bake for 10 to 30 minutes until the internal temperature reaches 160°F. Let rest for 15 minutes. If removing slices from the pan is difficult, run a knife around the edges and invert onto a cutting board or serving platter.

Exploded Pierogi Lasagna

Pierogi are dumplings often stuffed with potatoes, onions, and/or cheese, and this dish features all the same yummy flavors. When I cook pierogi, one or two invariably break open, and that goof gave me the idea to just layer them in a lasagna.

SERVES 6

SIMPLE CARAMELIZED ONIONS

3 tablespoons butter

2 large onions, quartered and sliced

6 lasagna noodles

MASHED POTATO FILLING

3 pounds yellow or russet potatoes, peeled and cut into large pieces

3 tablespoons butter

4 ounces cream cheese

1 cup whole milk

½ teaspoon fine sea salt

¼ teaspoon freshly ground black pepper

2 cups (8 ounces) shredded white cheddar cheese

Chopped fresh chives or green onions

MAKE THE SIMPLE CARAMELIZED ONIONS: Melt the butter in a large skillet over medium-low heat. Add the onions, stirring well. Cook for 30 to 40 minutes, stirring every 5 to 7 minutes, or until the onions are golden brown.

PREHEAT THE OVEN to 375°F. Lightly grease a 9 x 9-inch baking dish.

COOK THE LASAGNA NOODLES in boiling salted water according to the package directions. Drain, then rinse with cool water.

MAKE THE MASHED POTATO FILLING: Boil the potatoes in salted water to cover in a large pot for 10 minutes or until tender. Drain and transfer to a large bowl. Add the butter, cream cheese, milk, salt, and pepper, mashing and stirring until the mixture is well blended.

ASSEMBLE: Arrange half of the noodles in the bottom of the prepared baking dish, cutting to fit the pan. Top with half of the potatoes, half of the onions, and half of the cheese. Repeat with remaining noodles, potatoes, onions, and cheese.

COVER AND BAKE for 30 minutes. Uncover and bake for 20 minutes until golden brown. Let stand for 10 minutes before serving. Sprinkle with chopped fresh chives or green onions.

French Onion Lasagna

Yellow, white, or sweet onions are good choices for this recipe. In general, sweet onions are tender and may get a bit mushy with extended cooking, but their flavor is still nice. To keep your eyes from watering too much when slicing, refrigerate the onions first (but this isn't a guarantee).

~~~~~~~~~~~~~~~~~~~~~~~~~ **SERVES 4** ~~~~~~~~~~~~~~~~~~~~~~~~~

CARAMELIZED ONIONS

- 2 tablespoons extra-virgin olive oil
- 3 onions, halved and sliced
- 1 tablespoon butter
- 3 garlic cloves, minced
- 1 teaspoon fine sea salt

WHITE WINE PARMESAN SAUCE

- 2 tablespoons butter
- 2 tablespoons all-purpose flour
- ¼ cup white wine
- 2 cups whole milk or half and half
- ¼ teaspoon fine sea salt
- ¼ teaspoon freshly ground black pepper
- ¾ cup (3 ounces) shredded Parmesan cheese

- 6 to 9 oven-ready lasagna noodles
- ½ cup (2 ounces) shredded Swiss cheese
- ¼ cup Italian-seasoned panko breadcrumbs

PREHEAT THE OVEN to 350°F. Lightly grease an 8 x 8-inch or 9 x 9-inch baking dish.

MAKE THE CARAMELIZED ONIONS: Heat the oil in a large skillet over medium heat. Add the onions and cook, stirring frequently, for 10 minutes until translucent. Stir in the butter and garlic. Cook, stirring occasionally, for 30 to 40 minutes or until the onions are golden brown. Stir in the salt.

MAKE THE WHITE WINE PARMESAN SAUCE: Melt the butter in a large skillet over medium heat. Whisk in the flour and cook, stirring constantly, for 1 minute. Whisk in the milk, salt, and pepper. Cook, stirring frequently, for 5 minutes or until the mixture thickens. Stir in the Parmesan cheese.

ASSEMBLE: Spread ½ cup of the white sauce in the bottom of the prepared baking dish. Top with 2 to 3 noodles and one-third of the onion mixture. Repeat twice in this order: ½ cup of the white sauce, 2 to 3 noodles, and one-third of the onion mixture. Spread the remaining sauce over the onions and sprinkle evenly with the Swiss cheese and panko.

COVER AND BAKE for 25 minutes. Uncover and bake for 10 minutes until golden brown. Let stand for 10 minutes before serving.

VEGETARIAN

Fried Lasagna Bites

I'll openly admit that breading food in three stages and frying it is a bit of a pain. But it's necessary to get the right coating thickness and worth the hassle, since these crispy and delicious appetizers are a crowd pleaser. You can make them ahead of time and freeze either after folding into triangles or after breading. Just make sure to thaw them in the refrigerator before frying; if they're still frozen, the inside will be ice-cold while the outside is golden brown. I've tried them both fried immediately after rolling and then after a few days in the freezer, and the results are equally yummy.

〰〰〰〰〰〰〰〰 **SERVES 8 TO 16** 〰〰〰〰〰〰〰〰

1 (16-ounce) package lasagna noodles (about 16 noodles)

BASIL-RICOTTA FILLING

1 (15-ounce) container ricotta cheese

½ cup (2 ounces) shredded Parmesan cheese

1 large egg

2 tablespoons prepared pesto or chopped fresh basil or other herb

¼ teaspoon fine sea salt

¼ teaspoon freshly ground black pepper

Vegetable oil

¾ cup all-purpose flour

3 large eggs

1½ cup seasoned breadcrumbs

Warm pasta or marinara sauce

COOK THE LASAGNA NOODLES in boiling salted water according to the package directions. Drain, then rinse in cool water. Lay out on a baking sheet and cover with plastic wrap until ready to roll.

MAKE THE BASIL-RICOTTA FILLING: Combine the ricotta, Parmesan, egg, pesto, salt, and pepper in a bowl.

ASSEMBLE: Spread about 2 tablespoons of the filling evenly onto each lasagna noodle. Fold over diagonally about 3 inches, continuing to fold like a flag until a triangle is made. Cover and chill in the refrigerator or freezer for at least 1 hour until the filling is firm.

PLACE THE FLOUR in a shallow bowl. Beat the eggs with 2 tablespoons water in another shallow bowl. Place the breadcrumbs in a third shallow bowl.

DREDGE THE LASAGNA PIECES in the flour, then dip in the egg mixture, allowing any excess to drip off. Dredge in the breadcrumb mixture. (To make ahead, cover with plastic wrap and freeze for up to a week. Thaw before frying.)

POUR THE OIL to a depth of ½ inch in a deep, heavy skillet. Heat to 350°F. Fry the breaded pieces, seam side down, for 2 minutes. Turn over and fry another 2 minutes. Drain on paper towels. Serve with the warm sauce.

Easy Eggplant Parmesan Lasagna

Sometimes I get a craving, but there's just one element of a recipe that stops me from moving forward. One such roadblock is the breaded and fried eggplant in eggplant Parmesan. I love it, but I often simply stop and eat the fried slices of eggplant with a bit of sauce. In this dish, getting a head start with pre-breaded eggplant slices means you can save about an hour of prep. I still recommend baking the eggplant first to ensure the breading is browned and crisp. If you want to shortcut on another level, skip making the red sauce and use four cups of jarred pasta sauce.

~~~~~~~~ **SERVES 6** ~~~~~~~~

1 (16-ounce) package frozen and thawed breaded sliced eggplant

EASY RED SAUCE

1 tablespoon extra-virgin olive oil

1 onion, chopped

4 garlic cloves, minced

¼ teaspoon crushed red pepper flakes

1 (28-ounce) can crushed tomatoes with basil

2 tablespoons dry red or white wine

½ teaspoon sugar

RICOTTA FILLING

1 (15-ounce) container ricotta cheese

1 large egg

1 cup (4 ounces) shredded mozzarella cheese

¼ teaspoon fine sea salt

¼ teaspoon freshly ground black pepper

1 cup (4 ounces) shredded mozzarella cheese

½ cup (2 ounces) shredded or grated Romano or Parmesan cheese

¼ cup chopped fresh Italian parsley

PREHEAT THE OVEN to 425°F. Lightly grease a 9 x 9-inch or 8-cup baking dish.

PLACE THE EGGPLANT on a lightly greased baking sheet. Bake for 10 minutes. Remove and reduce the temperature to 350°F.

MAKE THE EASY RED SAUCE: Heat the oil in a large skillet over medium-high. Add the onion and cook, stirring frequently, for 5 minutes or until tender. Add the garlic and red pepper flakes and cook, stirring frequently, for 3 minutes. Stir in the crushed tomatoes, wine, and sugar. Cook, stirring occasionally, for 20 minutes.

MAKE THE RICOTTA FILLING: Combine the ricotta, egg, mozzarella cheese, salt, and pepper in a medium bowl.

ASSEMBLE: Spread 1 cup of the red sauce in the bottom of the prepared baking dish. Top with half of the eggplant, half of the ricotta filling, and half of the remaining sauce. Repeat with the remaining eggplant, ricotta, and sauce. Sprinkle the top with the mozzarella and Romano cheeses.

COVER AND BAKE for 25 minutes. Uncover and bake for 20 minutes until golden brown and bubbly. Let stand for 10 minutes before serving. Sprinkle with the parsley.

Super-Easy Ravioli Lasagna

When you want a cozy casserole that can be assembled in minutes, take a few shortcuts with store-bought ravioli. It's also a great starter recipe if you want the kiddos to help out with dinner. Cheese-filled ravioli is always available, but there are all sorts of interesting fillings to try like mushrooms, lobster, pesto, and so on.

~~~~~~~~~~ **SERVES 4** ~~~~~~~~~~

1 (9- or 10-ounce) package frozen chopped spinach, thawed

1 (24-ounce) jar pasta or marinara sauce, any flavor

1 (20-ounce) package refrigerated ravioli, any flavor

2 cups (8 ounces) shredded mozzarella cheese

1 cup (4 ounces) shredded Parmesan cheese

PREHEAT THE OVEN to 350°F. Lightly grease an 8-cup baking dish.

DRAIN THE SPINACH in a colander, then squeeze dry between paper towels to remove the excess liquid.

ASSEMBLE: Spread 1 cup of the pasta sauce in the bottom of the baking dish. Top with a layer of the ravioli, about one-third of the package. Spread one-third of the spinach over the ravioli. Sprinkle with one-third of the mozzarella cheese. Repeat twice in this order: sauce, ravioli, spinach, and mozzarella. Top the lasagna evenly with the Parmesan cheese.

COVER AND BAKE for 30 minutes. Uncover and bake for 15 minutes or broil for 3 to 5 minutes until golden brown and bubbly. Let stand for 10 minutes before serving.

VEGETARIAN

Spicy Cheese Volcano (aka "Pimiento & Cheese") Lasagna

I go through crushed red pepper flakes faster than you'd imagine since my daughter Corinne adds them to everything she makes. This creation is one of her interpretations and includes a lot of spices she insists remain in the recipe ("Because that's the volcano"). Still, my advice is that sensitive palates should swap the smoked paprika for the regular sweet kind and back off the red pepper flakes.

~~~~~~~~~~ **SERVES 4 TO 6** ~~~~~~~~~~

10 lasagna noodles

PIMIENTO SAUCE

1 (16-ounce) jar roasted red bell peppers, drained well

3 garlic cloves, minced

½ teaspoon smoked paprika

½ teaspoon fine sea salt

¼ teaspoon freshly ground black pepper

¼ teaspoon garlic powder

¼ teaspoon cayenne pepper

SPICY CHEDDAR CHEESE SAUCE

2 tablespoons butter

½ teaspoon crushed red pepper flakes

2 tablespoons all-purpose flour

2½ cups half and half

½ cup (2 ounces) shredded cheddar cheese

½ teaspoon chili powder

1 cup (4 ounces) shredded cheddar cheese

PREHEAT THE OVEN to 350°F. Lightly grease a 9 x 9-inch baking dish.

COOK THE LASAGNA NOODLES in boiling salted water according to the package directions. Drain, then rinse in cool water.

MAKE THE PIMIENTO SAUCE: Combine the bell peppers, garlic, smoked paprika, salt, pepper, garlic powder, and cayenne pepper in a food processor. Process until smooth.

MAKE THE SPICY CHEDDAR CHEESE SAUCE: Melt the butter and red pepper flakes in a large skillet over medium-high heat. Whisk in the flour and cook, stirring constantly, for 1 minute. Whisk in the half and half. Cook, stirring frequently, for 5 minutes until thickened. Add the cheddar and chili powder, stirring until the mixture is smooth.

ASSEMBLE: Spread 1 cup of the cheese sauce in the bottom of the prepared baking dish. Place the noodles on a flat surface. Spread each one with 1 to 1½ tablespoons of the Pimiento Sauce. Roll up and place, seam side down, on the sauce. Pour the remaining cheese sauce over the rolls. Sprinkle the top with the cheddar cheese. Dollop with any remaining Pimiento Sauce.

COVER AND BAKE for 20 minutes. Uncover and bake for 5 minutes or until lightly browned. Let stand for 10 minutes before serving.

Mac & Cheese-Inspired Lasagna

This version is what I call the "base" recipe. It's yummy on its own, but I like to add variations depending on who's coming to dinner. You can sneak in veggies by adding shredded carrots or zucchini to the cheese mix. Allow grated zucchini or summer squash to sit on paper towels for a few minutes to absorb excess water. Carnivores will appreciate a half pound or so of cooked ground beef or two cups of shredded rotisserie chicken. I've even added thinly sliced leftover flank steak and topped the entire thing with a few sliced tomatoes when the summer garden is bountiful.

~~~ **SERVES 10 TO 12** ~~~

1 (16-ounce) package lasagna noodles

THREE-CHEESE SAUCE
8 tablespoons (½ cup) salted butter

½ cup all-purpose flour

4 cups half and half

½ teaspoon fine sea salt

½ teaspoon garlic powder

¼ to ½ teaspoon cayenne pepper

4 cups (16 ounces) shredded sharp cheddar cheese

2 cups (8 ounces) shredded Gruyère cheese

1 cup (4 ounces) shredded Parmesan, Asiago, or Romano cheese

1 (15-ounce) container ricotta cheese (optional)

1 cup seasoned panko breadcrumbs

PREHEAT THE OVEN to 350°F. Lightly grease a 13 x 9-inch deep-dish baking dish.

COOK THE LASAGNA NOODLES in boiling salted water according to the package directions. Drain, then rinse in cool water.

MAKE THE THREE-CHEESE SAUCE: Melt the butter in a large saucepan over medium-high heat. Whisk in the flour and cook, stirring constantly, for 1 minute. Whisk in the half and half, salt, garlic powder, and cayenne pepper. Cook, stirring frequently, for 5 minutes. Add 3 cups of the cheddar cheese, whisking until it melts and the mixture is smooth. Add the Gruyère and Parmesan cheese, whisking until smooth.

ASSEMBLE: Spread 1 cup of the cheese sauce in the bottom of the prepared dish. Top with 4 lasagna noodles. Continue to layer 1 cup of cheese sauce and 4 noodles, ending with sauce on the top. If desired, spoon heaping teaspoon-size dollops of ricotta cheese sporadically around as you layer the noodles and cheese sauce. Sprinkle the top with the remaining 1 cup of cheddar cheese and the panko.

BAKE, UNCOVERED, for 30 minutes or until hot and bubbly. Let stand for 10 minutes before serving.

Corinne's Cherry Tomato & Arugula Lasagna

For the past year, my daughter Corinne has made herself a dinner of linguine topped with a cheesy cherry tomato sauce at least four times a week. She eagerly adapted her favorite pasta recipe into a lasagna. Corinne insists cherry tomatoes are the best, especially the multicolored ones, but you can substitute three large, coarsely chopped heirloom tomatoes.

SERVES 4

CHERRY TOMATO SAUCE

- 2 tablespoons extra-virgin olive oil
- ½ teaspoon crushed red pepper flakes
- 3 cups mixed cherry or grape tomatoes
- 4 garlic cloves, minced
- ¼ teaspoon fine sea salt
- ¼ teaspoon freshly ground black pepper
- 3 cups lightly packed baby arugula

PARMESAN BÉCHAMEL

- 2 tablespoons butter
- 2 tablespoons all-purpose flour
- 1½ cups whole milk or half and half
- ¼ teaspoon fine sea salt
- ¼ teaspoon freshly ground black pepper
- ½ cup (2 ounces) shredded Parmesan cheese

- 8 to 9 oven-ready lasagna noodles
- ½ cup (2 ounces) shredded mozzarella cheese
- ¼ cup Italian-seasoned panko breadcrumbs

PREHEAT THE OVEN to 375°F. Lightly grease an 8 x 8-inch or 9 x 9-inch baking dish.

MAKE THE CHERRY TOMATO SAUCE: Heat the oil and red pepper flakes in a large skillet over medium. Add the tomatoes and cook, stirring frequently, for 5 minutes or until they start to soften. Stir in the garlic, salt, and pepper. Cook, stirring frequently, for 5 minutes. Add the arugula and cook, tossing with tongs, for 3 to 5 minutes or until arugula wilts.

MAKE THE PARMESAN BÉCHAMEL: Melt the butter in a large skillet over medium heat. Whisk in the flour and cook, stirring constantly, for 1 minute. Whisk in the milk, salt, and pepper. Cook, stirring frequently, for 5 minutes or until the mixture thickens. Stir in the Parmesan cheese.

SPREAD ½ CUP OF THE BÉCHAMEL SAUCE in the bottom of the prepared baking dish. Top with 2 to 3 noodles, breaking into pieces to fit the pan. Spread with half of the cherry tomato sauce and half of the béchamel sauce. Repeat with the remaining noodles, tomato sauce, and béchamel sauce. Sprinkle the top with the mozzarella and panko.

COVER AND BAKE for 25 minutes. Uncover and bake for 10 to 15 minutes or until golden brown and bubbly. Let stand for 10 minutes before serving.

Veggie Walnut Superfood Lasagna

If lentil lasagna noodles aren't unavailable, substitute gluten-free or whole-grain noodles (and it's also okay to skip the noodles altogether). For the "cleanest" casserole, buy organic vegetables, particularly the kale and bell peppers. You'll find different types of quinoa—white, black, red, or multicolored. Choose your favorite. Remember to rinse the quinoa to remove the natural bitter coating that helps repel insects in the field.

〜〜〜〜〜〜〜〜〜〜〜〜〜 **SERVES 4 TO 6** 〜〜〜〜〜〜〜

2 cups vegetable broth

1 cup quinoa

3 large sweet potatoes (about 1½ pounds)

MISO-KALE MARINARA SAUCE

2 tablespoons avocado or extra-virgin olive oil

1 onion, chopped

1 red bell pepper, chopped

¼ teaspoon crushed red pepper

3 garlic cloves, minced

1 (28-ounce) can crushed tomatoes

2 tablespoons miso paste

6 cups (5 ounces) lightly packed baby kale

8 oven-ready green lentil or whole-grain lasagna noodles

1 cup (4 ounces) crumbled feta, shredded Parmesan, or shredded mozzarella cheese

⅔ cup chopped walnuts

PREHEAT THE OVEN to 350°F. Lightly grease a 9 x 9-inch baking dish.

COMBINE THE BROTH and the quinoa in a medium saucepan. Bring to a boil over medium-high heat. Reduce the heat to medium-low, cover, and simmer for 15 minutes or until the quinoa is tender. Stir with a fork to fluff.

MICROWAVE THE SWEET POTATOES for 5 to 6 minutes until halfway cooked. Set aside until cool enough to handle. Peel and slice ⅛ inch thick.

MAKE THE MISO-KALE MARINARA SAUCE: Heat the oil in a large skillet over medium-high. Add the onion, bell pepper, and red pepper flakes. Cook, stirring occasionally, for 5 minutes. Add the garlic and cook for 1 minute. Stir in the tomatoes and miso paste. Cook, stirring frequently, for 10 minutes. Stir in the kale and cook, stirring occasionally, for 5 to 7 minutes or until the kale is cooked into the sauce.

ASSEMBLE: Spread ½ cup of the marinara sauce in the bottom of the prepared dish. Top with 4 noodles. Arrange half of the sweet potatoes over the noodles and top with half of the quinoa and half of the marinara sauce. Repeat with the remaining noodles, sweet potatoes, quinoa, and marinara. Sprinkle with feta cheese and walnuts.

COVER AND BAKE for 45 minutes. Uncover and bake for 10 minutes until golden brown. Let stand for 10 minutes before serving.

Ratatouille Lasagna

This celebration of our favorite summer veggies makes a satisfying vegetarian main dish, or as a side dish for grilled chicken or ribs. Use a three-inch-deep casserole dish or a roasting pan since the plentiful mixture might bubble over the sides, especially if your summer squash and eggplant are on the big side. I gave a wide range for the noodles; I don't want them overpowering the vegetables, but some may want the extra pasta. Slip a knife into center areas to make sure the no-boil noodles have cooked to a tender consistency.

SERVES 10

VEGGIE PASTA SAUCE

2 tablespoons extra-virgin olive oil

1 onion, chopped

2 bell peppers, seeded and diced

3 carrots, chopped

1 (8-ounce) package button or cremini mushrooms, sliced

5 garlic cloves, minced

¼ teaspoon crushed red pepper flakes

1 (24-ounce) jar pasta or marinara sauce

¼ cup chopped sun-dried tomatoes in oil

HERBED RICOTTA FILLING

1 (15-ounce) container ricotta cheese

1 cup (4 ounces) shredded mozzarella cheese

1 cup (4 ounces) shredded or grated Parmesan or Romano cheese

1 large egg

¼ cup chopped fresh basil

2 tablespoons chopped fresh parsley

½ teaspoon fine sea salt

½ teaspoon freshly ground black pepper

6 to 10 oven-ready lasagna noodles

1 small eggplant, thinly sliced (peeled if desired)

1 zucchini, thinly sliced

1 yellow squash, thinly sliced

2 red or yellow tomatoes, thinly sliced and seeded

1 cup (4 ounces) shredded mozzarella cheese

½ cup (2 ounces) shredded or grated Parmesan or Romano Cheese

PREHEAT THE OVEN to 375°F. Lightly grease a deep 13 x 9-inch baking dish.

MAKE THE VEGGIE PASTA SAUCE: Heat the oil in a large skillet over medium-high. Add the onion, bell peppers, carrots, mushrooms, garlic, and red pepper flakes. Cook for 10 minutes, stirring frequently, or until the vegetables are tender. Stir in the pasta sauce and sun-dried tomatoes.

MAKE THE HERBED RICOTTA FILLING: Combine the ricotta, mozzarella, Parmesan, egg, basil, parsley, salt, and pepper in a bowl.

ASSEMBLE: Spoon 1 cup of the pasta sauce in the bottom of the prepared dish. Top with 3 to 5 noodles, breaking to fit the pan, if necessary. Top with half of the sauce and half of the ricotta filling. Layer half of the eggplant, zucchini, squash, and tomatoes overlapping each about halfway over the previous slice. Repeat with the remaining noodles, sauce, ricotta, and sliced vegetables.

COVER AND BAKE for 45 to 50 minutes or until the center is hot. Uncover and sprinkle the top with the mozzarella and Parmesan cheeses. Bake for 15 minutes or broil for 3 to 5 minutes until the cheese melts. Let stand for 10 minutes before serving.

Spring Sweet Pea & Asparagus Lasagna

Few things herald the start of warm spring days than seeing bundles of thin asparagus taking the place of cauliflower on tables at the farmers' market. Since this recipe is so veggie heavy, I placed it with the other vegetarian recipes even with the option of adding a bit of salty pancetta. Luckily this recipe works just fine with off-season or frozen veggies, so enjoy it when you need a break from winter foods.

~~~~~~~~ **SERVES 8** ~~~~~~~~

2 (1-pound) bunches asparagus, trimmed

RICOTTA–BABY PEA FILLING

4 cups fresh or frozen and thawed baby or English peas

¼ cup vegetable broth

¼ teaspoon fine sea salt

1 (15-ounce) container ricotta cheese

1 large egg

PANCETTA-LEEK WHITE SAUCE

2 tablespoons butter

1 large leek, sliced, or 2 shallots, minced

½ cup coarsely chopped pancetta, bacon, or prosciutto (optional)

3 tablespoons all-purpose flour

2 cups half and half or whole milk

1 cup vegetable broth

¼ teaspoon ground nutmeg

½ cup (2 ounces) shredded Parmesan cheese, divided

12 oven-ready lasagna noodles

¼ cup panko breadcrumbs

¼ cup sliced almonds

2 teaspoons chopped fresh thyme

PREHEAT YOUR OVEN to 350°F. Lightly grease a 13 x 9-inch baking dish.

BRING A POT OF SALTED WATER TO BOIL. Add the asparagus and cook for 5 minutes until just barely tender. Remove with tongs or a slotted spoon and set aside. Keep the water boiling.

MAKE THE RICOTTA–BABY PEA FILLING: Add the peas to the boiling water and cook for 5 to 8 minutes until tender. Drain in a colander, then rinse with cold water to cool. Set aside 2 cups of the peas. Place 2 cups of the remaining peas in a food processor. Add the broth and salt and process until smooth. Transfer to a large bowl. Stir in the ricotta, egg, and the reserved 2 cups blanched peas.

MAKE THE PANCETTA-LEEK WHITE SAUCE: Melt the butter in a large skillet over medium-high heat. Add the leek and pancetta, if using, and cook, stirring frequently, for 3 minutes until the leek is tender and the pancetta is cooked. Whisk in the flour and cook, stirring constantly, for 1 minute. Whisk in the milk, broth, and nutmeg. Cook, stirring frequently, for 5 minutes or until the mixture thickens. Stir in ¼ cup of the Parmesan cheese.

ASSEMBLE: Spread ½ cup of the white sauce in the bottom of the prepared baking dish. Layer in this order: 4 noodles, half of the ricotta filling, 4 noodles, one-third of the white sauce, half of the asparagus, the remaining ricotta filling, 4 noodles, one-third of the sauce, the remaining asparagus and white sauce. Sprinkle the top with the remaining ¼ cup Parmesan, the breadcrumbs, almonds, and thyme.

COVER AND BAKE for 30 minutes. Uncover and bake for 20 minutes or until golden brown and bubbly. Let stand for 10 minutes before serving.

Vegan "Ricotta" & Spinach Lasagna

Anytime you want to skip ricotta because you are eating dairy-free, consider making a batch of this tofu-based substitute. The miso paste adds a rich umami flavor—I prefer white miso, but any other flavors works in the recipe, although dark miso will tint the "ricotta" a deeper shade.

~~~~~~~~~~~~ **SERVES 4** ~~~~~~~~~~~~

TOFU "RICOTTA" WITH SPINACH

- 1 (16-ounce) package soft tofu, drained
- ¼ cup unsweetened almond, soy, or coconut milk
- 2 tablespoons nutritional yeast
- 2 teaspoons fresh lemon juice
- 2 tablespoons white miso paste
- 1 (9- to 12-ounce) package frozen spinach, thawed and drained well
- Fine sea salt and freshly ground black pepper

- 1 (24-ounce) jar pasta or marinara sauce
- 9 brown rice or gluten-free, oven-ready lasagna noodles
- 1 (7-ounce) package dairy-free mozzarella cheese

PREHEAT THE OVEN to 350°F. Lightly grease an 8 x 8-inch baking dish.

MAKE THE TOFU "RICOTTA" WITH SPINACH: Combine the tofu, almond milk, nutritional yeast, lemon juice, and miso paste in a large bowl. Mash with a fork until well blended. Stir in the spinach. Taste and season with salt and pepper.

ASSEMBLE: Spread 1 cup of the sauce on the bottom of the prepared baking dish. Top with 3 noodles, one-third of the tofu mixture, and one-third of the remaining sauce. Repeat twice with 3 noodles, one-third tofu, and one-third sauce. Sprinkle with the mozzarella cheese.

COVER AND BAKE for 30 minutes. Uncover and bake for another 25 minutes. Let stand for 10 minutes before serving.

Vegan & Gluten-Free Chickpea & Yellow Squash Lasagna

Chickpeas (also called garbanzo beans) offer the same toothy texture as finely ground beef when blended with seasoned tomatoes and fresh herbs. They are a good source of protein while providing lots of healthy fiber. (Bonus: They are less expensive than meat or packed meat substitutes!)

~~~~~~~~~~~ SERVES 4 ~~~~~~~~~~~

CHICKPEA PASTA SAUCE

- 2 (15-ounce) cans chickpeas or garbanzo beans, rinsed and drained
- 1 (14-ounce) can seasoned diced tomatoes, undrained
- ⅓ cup lightly packed fresh basil
- ½ teaspoon fine sea salt
- ¼ teaspoon freshly ground pepper

SPICED GLUTEN- & DAIRY-FREE WHITE SAUCE

- 2 tablespoons extra-virgin olive oil
- 2 tablespoons gluten-free flour blend
- 2 cups coconut or soy milk or 1 (13.5-ounce) can coconut milk
- ½ teaspoon fine sea salt
- ¼ teaspoon freshly ground black pepper
- ¼ teaspoon garam masala or curry powder

- 1 tablespoon extra-virgin olive oil
- 1 onion, halved and sliced
- ¼ teaspoon crushed red pepper flakes
- 1 large or 2 small yellow squash, sliced
- 8 gluten-free lasagna noodles
- 1 (7-ounce) package dairy-free mozzarella cheese

PREHEAT THE OVEN to 350°F. Lightly grease a 13 x 9-baking dish.

MAKE THE CHICKPEA PASTA SAUCE: Combine the chickpeas, tomatoes, basil, salt, and pepper in a blender or food processor. Blend or process until finely chopped.

MAKE THE SPICED GLUTEN- AND DAIRY-FREE WHITE SAUCE: Heat the oil in a large skillet over medium. Whisk in the gluten-free flour blend and cook, stirring constantly, for 3 to 5 minutes until the mixture turns a pale golden color. Whisk in the coconut milk and cook, stirring frequently, for 5 minutes or until the mixture thickens. Stir in the salt, pepper, and garam masala. (Taste a small amount and add more spice, if desired.)

HEAT THE TABLESPOON OIL in a large skillet over medium-high heat. Add the onion and red pepper flakes and cook, stirring frequently, for 5 minutes until the onion is tender. Add the squash and cook, stirring occasionally, for 5 minutes or until tender.

ASSEMBLE: Spoon 1 cup of the chickpea sauce in the bottom of the prepared dish. Top with 4 noodles, breaking to fit the pan. Layer with half of the squash mixture, half of the remaining chickpea sauce, and half of the white sauce. Repeat with 4 noodles, the remaining squash, chickpea sauce, and white sauce. Sprinkle with the mozzarella.

COVER AND BAKE for 30 minutes. Uncover and bake for another 10 minutes until golden and bubbly. Let stand for 10 minutes before serving.

VEGETARIAN

SEAFOOD

Langostino Lasagna alla Vodka

Langostinos are a shellfish that resemble and taste similar to crawfish or tiny lobsters. You can find them precooked and IQF (individually quick frozen), and they only require a few minutes in the skillet to heat through. Feel free to substitute peeled and deveined shrimp. Although a small amount, the vodka in this creamy tomato sauce is a key ingredient. The alcohol helps emulsify the liquids and fats in the sauce while enhancing the taste and aroma without being obvious.

〰〰〰〰〰〰〰 **SERVES 8** 〰〰〰〰〰〰〰

VODKA SAUCE

- 2 tablespoons extra-virgin olive oil
- 1 sweet onion, chopped
- ¼ teaspoon crushed red pepper flakes
- 3 garlic cloves, minced
- ⅓ cup vodka
- 1 (28-ounce) can crushed tomatoes with basil
- ½ cup heavy cream
- 1 tablespoon tomato paste
- 1 tablespoon balsamic vinegar
- 1 teaspoon sugar
- ¼ teaspoon fine sea salt
- ½ cup (2 ounces) grated Parmesan cheese

RICOTTA FILLING

- 1 (15-ounce) container ricotta cheese
- 1 cup (4 ounces) shredded Parmesan cheese
- 1 large egg
- ¼ teaspoon fine sea salt
- ¼ teaspoon freshly ground black pepper

- 2 tablespoons butter
- 3 garlic cloves, minced
- 2 pounds cooked langostino tail meat
- 1 teaspoon Italian or seafood seasoning
- ¼ teaspoon fine sea salt
- 8 to 10 oven-ready lasagna noodles
- 2 cups (8 ounces) shredded mozzarella cheese
- 2 tablespoons chopped fresh basil
- ¼ teaspoon freshly ground black pepper

PREHEAT THE OVEN to 350°F. Lightly grease a 13 x 9-inch baking dish.

MAKE THE VODKA SAUCE: Heat the olive oil in a large skillet over medium-high. Add the onion and red pepper flakes and cook, stirring frequently, for 5 minutes or until tender. Stir in the garlic and cook, stirring frequently, for 2 minutes. Add the vodka and cook, stirring frequently, for 1 minute or until most of the liquid evaporates. Stir in the tomatoes, cream, tomato paste, vinegar, sugar, and salt. Bring the mixture to a boil, reduce the heat to medium-low, and simmer for 15 to 20 minutes. Add the Parmesan cheese, stirring until smooth.

MAKE THE RICOTTA FILLING: Combine the ricotta, Parmesan, egg, salt, and pepper in a bowl.

MELT THE BUTTER in a large skillet over medium-high heat. Add the garlic, langostinos, and Italian seasoning. Cook, stirring occasionally, for 5 to 7 minutes or until the langostinos are cooked through.

ASSEMBLE: Spoon ½ cup of the sauce into the bottom of the baking dish. Top with 3 to 4 noodles, breaking to fit the dish. Top with half the ricotta filling, half the langostinos, and half the remaining sauce. Repeat with 3 to 4 noodles, the remaining ricotta, langostinos, and sauce. Sprinkle with the mozzarella cheese.

COVER AND BAKE for 30 minutes. Let stand for 10 minutes before serving. Sprinkle with the chopped fresh basil and black pepper.

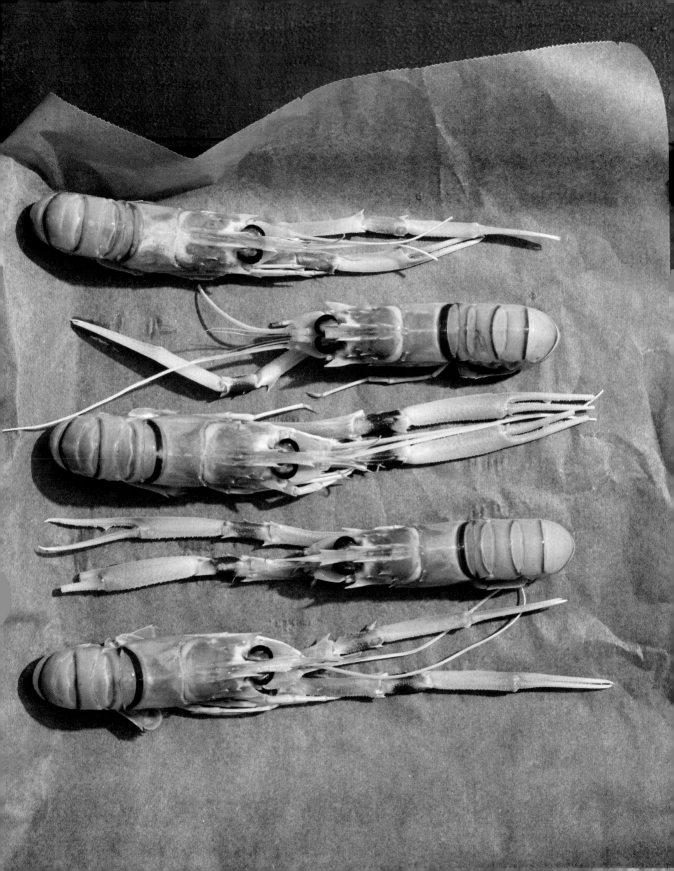

Shrimp Enchiladas
with Spicy Jack Cheese Sauce

Green salsa is also known as salsa verde. It's usually made
with green tomatillos and has a tart, herby flavor, and it is sold
in a variety of heat levels. I've sometimes made this family favorite
with prepared guacamole salsa instead of plain salsa verde,
and the results are equally as delicious.

SERVES 8

1 tablespoon extra-virgin
olive oil

1 onion, finely chopped

1½ pounds raw small shrimp,
peeled and deveined

3 garlic cloves, minced

1 teaspoon ground cumin

½ teaspoon fine sea salt

1 (4-ounce) can diced green
chilies

½ cup chopped fresh cilantro

1 tablespoon fresh lime juice

SPICY JACK CHEESE SAUCE

1½ tablespoons butter

1½ tablespoons all-purpose
flour

½ teaspoon ground cumin

¼ teaspoon fine sea salt

1 cup chicken broth

1 cup salsa verde

1 cup (4 ounces) shredded
Pepper Jack cheese

8 (6-inch) corn tortillas

2 tablespoons fresh cilantro
leaves

2 tablespoons toasted
pumpkin seeds or pepitas

PREHEAT THE OVEN to
375°F. Lightly grease an
8-cup baking dish.

HEAT THE OIL in a large skillet
over medium-high heat. Add
the onion and cook, stirring
frequently, for 3 to 5 minutes
or until tender. Add the shrimp,
garlic, cumin, and salt. Cook,
stirring frequently, for 5 minutes
or until the shrimp are cooked
through. Stir in the green chilies,
cilantro, and lime juice.

**MAKE THE SPICY JACK
CHEESE SAUCE:** Melt the butter
in a skillet over medium-high
heat. Whisk in the flour, cumin,
and salt and cook, stirring
constantly, for 1 minute. Whisk
in the broth and cook, stirring
frequently, for 3 to 4 minutes
or until thickened. Add the salsa
and cheese, stirring until well
blended and smooth.

ASSEMBLE: Spread ½ cup
of the cheese sauce in the
bottom of the prepared baking
dish. Arrange 4 of the tortillas,
tearing them to fit in a single
layer. Top with half the shrimp
mixture and half the sauce.
Repeat with the remaining
tortillas, shrimp mixture,
and sauce.

COVER AND BAKE for
25 minutes. Let stand for
10 minutes before serving.
Top with the cilantro and
toasted pumpkin seeds.

SEAFOOD

Shrimp & Garlic Scampi Lasagna

Make this simple yet crave-worthy lasagna to satisfy your seafood-and-pasta fix. Bump up the red pepper flakes for more heat. Adding the eggs to the wine sauce adds body and a silky texture to the zesty sauce.

~~~~~~~~~~ **SERVES 4 TO 6** ~~~~~~~~~~

- 1 tablespoon extra-virgin olive oil
- 2 tablespoons butter
- ⅛ teaspoon crushed red pepper flakes
- 5 garlic cloves, minced
- 2 pounds large shrimp, peeled and deveined

LEMON-WINE SAUCE
- 2 tablespoons butter
- 3 tablespoons all-purpose flour
- ½ cup white wine
- 2 cups shrimp or vegetable broth
- ½ cup half and half or heavy cream
- ¼ teaspoon fine sea salt
- 2 tablespoons fresh lemon juice
- ¼ cup chopped fresh parsley
- 2 large eggs

- 6 oven-ready lasagna noodles
- 1 cup (4 ounces) shredded Romano or Parmesan cheese
- Chopped fresh parsley

PREHEAT THE OVEN to 350°F. Lightly grease a 9 x 9-inch baking dish.

HEAT THE OIL and butter in a large skillet over medium. Add the crushed red pepper flakes and garlic and cook for 1 minute. Add the shrimp and cook, stirring occasionally, for 5 to 7 minutes until they are just done. Transfer to a bowl. Reserve the skillet.

MAKE THE LEMON-WINE SAUCE: Melt the butter in the skillet over medium heat. Whisk in the flour and cook, stirring constantly, for 1 minute. Whisk in the wine and cook until it evaporates. Stir in the broth, half and half, and salt. Cook, stirring frequently, for 5 to 7 minutes or until thickened. Remove from the heat. Stir in the lemon juice and parsley. Whisk the eggs in a small bowl. Temper the eggs by drizzling about 1 cup of the hot lemon-wine mixture into the bowl with the eggs while whisking constantly. Pour the egg mixture into the skillet with the sauce mixture and whisk until well blended.

ASSEMBLE: Spread ½ cup of the lemon-wine sauce in the bottom of the prepared dish. Top with 3 noodles, breaking to fit. Top the noodles with half the shrimp, half the sauce, and half the Romano cheese. Repeat with 3 more noodles and the remaining shrimp, sauce, and cheese.

COVER AND BAKE for 30 minutes. Uncover and broil for 3 to 5 minutes or until golden brown and bubbly. Let stand for 10 minutes before serving. Sprinkle with the parsley.

Seafood Au Gratin Lasagna

The size of the shrimp isn't indicated in this recipe because any size can be used. If you have very large shrimp, you might want to split them in half so you'll have a piece in every bite. Jumbo lump crab is the gold standard, but it's pricey and not necessary in this recipe. However, the less you spend on crabmeat, the more you'll need to pick through to catch small shell pieces.

SERVES 8

SEAFOOD FILLING

3 tablespoons butter

½ onion, chopped

2 garlic cloves, minced

1 pound shrimp, peeled and deveined

½ pound bay scallops

1 pound crabmeat or cooked lobster meat, picked for shells

2 tablespoons chopped Italian parsley

SEAFOOD BÉCHAMEL

2 tablespoons butter

3 tablespoons all-purpose flour

¼ cup white wine

1 cup seafood broth, clam juice, or vegetable broth

2 cups half and half

1 tablespoon fresh lemon juice

1 teaspoon hot sauce

1 cup (4 ounces) shredded cheddar cheese

12 to 15 oven-ready lasagna noodles

⅔ cup seasoned panko breadcrumbs

1 cup (4 ounces) shredded cheddar cheese

¼ cup (1 ounce) shredded or grated Romano or Parmesan cheese

2 tablespoons butter, melted

PREHEAT THE OVEN to 350°F. Lightly grease a 13 x 9-inch baking dish.

MAKE THE SEAFOOD FILLING: Melt the butter in a large skillet over medium-high heat. Add the onion and cook for 3 to 5 minutes or until the onion is tender. Add the garlic, shrimp, and scallops and cook, stirring occasionally, for 5 to 7 minutes or until the shrimp and scallops are just done. Stir in the crab or lobster and parsley. Transfer to a bowl. Reserve the skillet.

MAKE THE SEAFOOD BÉCHAMEL: Melt the butter in the same large skillet over medium-high heat. Whisk in the flour and cook, stirring constantly, for 1 minute. Whisk in the wine and cook for 1 minute. Whisk in the broth, half and half, lemon juice, and hot sauce. Cook, stirring frequently, for 5 minutes or until the mixture thickens. Add the cheddar cheese and cook, stirring constantly, until smooth.

ASSEMBLE: Spread ¼ cup of the seafood sauce in the bottom of the prepared pan. Arrange 4 to 5 noodles over the sauce, breaking to fit the dish. Spoon one-third of the seafood filling over the noodles with a slotted spoon and top with one-third of the remaining sauce. Repeat twice in this order: 4 to 5 noodles, one-third of the seafood, one-third of the sauce.

COMBINE THE PANKO, cheddar, Romano, and melted butter in a small bowl. Sprinkle over the lasagna.

COVER AND BAKE for 40 minutes. Uncover and bake for 15 minutes until golden brown. Let stand for 10 minutes before serving.

SEAFOOD

Seafood with Goat Cheese Lasagna

Soft goat cheese is one of my all-time favorite cheeses, and I buy it in bulk every month. Its guaranteed presence in my refrigerator means it gets added experimentally to all types of recipes. I find it makes an interesting pairing with seafood by adding an earthy flavor with easy meltability. Not a fan? No worries—skip it or just substitute a cup of shredded Gouda.

SERVES 8

SHRIMP & SCALLOP FILLING

- 1 tablespoon extra-virgin olive oil
- 1 (8-ounce) package mushrooms, sliced
- 1 shallot, chopped
- 1 tablespoon chopped fresh thyme
- ½ teaspoon seafood seasoning or fine sea salt
- 1 pound medium shrimp, peeled and deveined
- ½ pound bay scallops
- ¼ cup white wine

BASIL–GOAT CHEESE BÉCHAMEL SAUCE

- 2 tablespoons butter
- 2 tablespoons all-purpose flour
- 2 cups half and half or whole milk
- 5 ounces crumbled goat or feta cheese
- ¼ cup chopped fresh basil
- ½ teaspoon seafood seasoning or fine sea salt

- 6 oven-ready lasagna noodles
- 1 cup (4 ounces) shredded mozzarella cheese
- ½ cup (2 ounces) shredded Parmesan cheese

PREHEAT THE OVEN to 375°F. Lightly grease a 9 x 9-inch or 8-cup baking dish.

MAKE THE SHRIMP AND SCALLOP FILLING: Heat the oil in a large skillet over medium heat. Add the mushrooms, shallot, thyme, and seafood seasoning. Cook, stirring frequently, for 8 minutes or until the mushrooms are tender. Add the shrimp and scallops and cook for 7 to 10 minutes or until the seafood is done. Add the wine and cook for 5 minutes or until it reduces.

MAKE THE BASIL–GOAT CHEESE BÉCHAMEL SAUCE: Melt the butter in a large skillet over medium heat. Whisk in the flour and cook, stirring constantly, for 1 minute. Whisk in the half and half and cook, stirring frequently, for 5 minutes or until the sauce thickens. Add the goat cheese, basil, and seafood seasoning, stirring until smooth.

ASSEMBLE: Spread ½ cup sauce in the bottom of the prepared pan. Arrange 3 noodles over the sauce, breaking some noodles to fit into the pan. Spoon half the seafood mixture over the noodles, drizzle evenly with half the remaining sauce, and sprinkle with half the mozzarella and Parmesan cheeses. Repeat with the remaining noodles, seafood, sauce, and cheeses.

COVER AND BAKE for 35 minutes. Uncover and bake for another 20 minutes or until golden brown and bubbly. Let stand for 10 minutes before serving.

Seafood Étouffée Lasagna

Large shrimp are the easiest to peel and devein, but they're large and lumpy in lasagnas. You can still use them, however—just slice them in half lengthwise after peeling so they lie flat. This will also help them to more easily spread in an even layer. Add uncooked seafood like oysters, scallops, or crawfish to the shrimp. Cooked crab and crawfish can be stirred in after the raw seafood is cooked. Cajun and Creole seasoning share many of the same flavors, but the Cajun blends are spicier while Creole blends highlight herbs.

SERVES 8

12 to 15 lasagna noodles

SEAFOOD FILLING

2 tablespoons extra-virgin olive oil

1 onion, chopped

1 green bell pepper, chopped

2 celery stalks, chopped

3 garlic cloves, minced

1 pound shrimp, peeled and deveined

1 pound crawfish, crab, oysters, or scallops, or a mix of any

½ teaspoon smoked paprika

¼ teaspoon fine sea salt

¼ teaspoon freshly ground pepper

CAJUN BÉCHAMEL SAUCE

3 tablespoons butter

3 tablespoons all-purpose flour

1 cup seafood stock or broth

1½ cups half and half or whole milk

1 tablespoon Cajun or Creole seasoning blend

½ cup (2 ounces) shredded Parmesan cheese

3 tablespoons chopped fresh parsley

2 cups (8 ounces) shredded mozzarella cheese

3 green onions, chopped

PREHEAT THE OVEN to 375°F. Lightly grease a 13 x 9-inch baking dish.

COOK THE LASAGNA NOODLES in boiling salted water according to the package directions. Drain, then rinse in cool water.

MAKE THE SEAFOOD FILLING: Heat the olive oil in a large skillet over medium-high heat. Add the onion, bell pepper, and celery. Cook, stirring frequently, for 5 minutes until tender. Add the garlic and cook for 1 minute. Add the shrimp, additional seafood (if using), paprika, salt, and pepper. Cook, stirring frequently, for 5 to 7 minutes or until shrimp are just done. Stir in cooked crawfish or crab, if using. Transfer to a bowl.

MAKE THE CAJUN BÉCHAMEL SAUCE: Melt the butter in a large skillet over medium-high heat. Whisk in the flour. Cook, stirring constantly, for 1 minute. Whisk in the broth, half and half, and Cajun blend. Cook, stirring frequently, for 5 minutes or until thickened. Add the Parmesan and parsley, stirring until smooth.

ASSEMBLE: Spread ½ cup of the béchamel sauce in the bottom of the prepared dish. Top with 4 or 5 noodles and one-third of the shrimp mixture, one-third of the remaining béchamel sauce, and one-third of the mozzarella cheese. Repeat twice in this order: noodles, shrimp mixture, béchamel, and mozzarella.

COVER AND BAKE for 30 minutes. Uncover and bake for 15 minutes until golden brown and bubbly. Let stand for 10 minutes before serving. Sprinkle with green onions.

Lemon Salmon Florentine Lasagna

Living a couple thousand miles away from Alaska or the Pacific Northwest, I know I'm probably not seeing fresh wild salmon in the grocery case. But no worries, I prefer buying frozen wild salmon and will ask for a frozen fillet (from the back freezer). Buying it frozen guarantees you have the freshest fish, but you will need to remove pin bones with pliers or a seafood tweezer. To thaw, remove the plastic packaging, cover with paper towels, and let stand in the refrigerator for several hours. If you buy thawed salmon at the market, ask that it was very recently thawed and not sitting in the case for more than a day.

〰️〰️〰️ **SERVES 4 TO 6** 〰️〰️〰️

2 tablespoons extra-virgin olive oil

2 garlic cloves, minced

1 (10-ounce) container baby spinach leaves

½ teaspoon fine sea salt

¼ teaspoon freshly ground black pepper

LEMON–CREAM CHEESE BÉCHAMEL SAUCE

3 tablespoons butter

2 tablespoons all-purpose flour

2 cups half and half

4 ounces cream cheese, softened

¼ teaspoon lemon zest

1 tablespoon fresh lemon juice

¼ teaspoon fine sea salt

1½ pounds boneless, skinless sockeye or king salmon filet, sliced horizontally into ¼-inch-thick pieces

6 to 9 oven-ready lasagna noodles

1 cup (4 ounces) shredded Parmesan cheese

PREHEAT THE OVEN to 350°F. Lightly grease an 8 x 8-inch or 9 x 9-inch baking dish.

HEAT THE OLIVE OIL in a large skillet over medium heat. Add the garlic and cook for 1 minute. Add the spinach, cover, and cook for 3 to 5 minutes, tossing occasionally with tongs, until it wilts. Add the salt and pepper and toss. Transfer to a bowl. Reserve the skillet.

MAKE THE LEMON–CREAM CHEESE BÉCHAMEL SAUCE: Melt the butter in the same skillet over medium-high heat. Whisk in the flour and cook, stirring constantly, for 1 minute. Whisk in the half and half and cook, stirring frequently, for 5 minutes or until the mixture thickens. Stir in the cream cheese, lemon zest and juice, and salt. Cook, stirring occasionally, for 3 minutes or until the mixture is smooth.

ASSEMBLE: Spoon ½ cup of the béchamel sauce into the bottom of the prepared baking dish. Arrange 2 to 3 noodles over the sauce, breaking the noodles to fit the pan. Top with one-third of the remaining sauce and half the spinach. Top with 2 to 3 noodles. Arrange all of the salmon over the noodles. Top with one-third of the sauce, the remaining half of the spinach, 2 to 3 noodles, and the remaining sauce. Sprinkle the top with Parmesan cheese.

COVER AND BAKE for 30 minutes or until the salmon is done. Uncover and broil for 3 minutes or until the top is golden brown and bubbly. Let stand for 10 minutes before serving.

Smoked Salmon, Potato & Watercress Lasagna

The small, round leaves on watercress have a spicy-peppery flavor. And like its cousins in the Brassicaceae family, watercress is packed with healthy nutrients. If you can't find it, use baby arugula, as it has a similar yet milder flavor. I prefer hot smoked salmon since the firm texture is easy to crumble, but you can use the softer sliced cold smoked salmon. You don't need much of the richly flavored fish to season this dish, but hard-core pescatarians can double or triple the amount of smoked salmon if you are lucky to have a large amount.

〜〜〜〜〜〜 **SERVES 4** 〜〜〜〜〜〜

3 Yukon gold, butter, or red potatoes (1¼ pounds), peeled if desired

WATERCRESS-CHEESE SAUCE
2 tablespoons butter

¼ red onion, finely chopped

2 tablespoons all-purpose flour

2 cups half and half

4 ounces cream cheese, softened, or crème fraiche

1 (4-ounce) container fresh watercress or baby arugula

2 tablespoons chopped fresh basil

2 teaspoons chopped fresh or ½ teaspoon dried dill

½ teaspoon fine sea salt

¼ teaspoon freshly ground black pepper

6 oven-ready lasagna noodles

1 (4-ounce) package smoked sockeye, coho, or king salmon

½ cup (2 ounces) shredded Parmesan cheese

PREHEAT THE OVEN to 350°F. Lightly grease an 8 x 8-inch baking dish.

MICROWAVE THE POTATOES for 3 to 5 minutes until almost cooked but still firm in the center. Let stand until cool enough to handle. Thinly slice.

MAKE THE WATERCRESS-CHEESE SAUCE: Melt the butter in a large skillet over medium-high heat. Add the onion and cook, stirring frequently, for 3 minutes or until tender. Whisk in the flour and cook, stirring constantly, for 1 minute. Whisk in the half and half and cook, stirring frequently, for 5 minutes or until the mixture thickens. Add the cream cheese and cook, stirring occasionally, until it melts and the mixture is smooth. Stir in the watercress, basil, dill, salt, and pepper.

ASSEMBLE: Spoon ½ cup of the watercress sauce into the bottom of the prepared dish. Top with 3 lasagna noodles, breaking some noodles to fit the pan. Top with half of the potatoes, half of the salmon, and half of the remaining watercress sauce. Repeat with 3 noodles, the remaining potatoes, salmon, and sauce. Sprinkle the top with the Parmesan cheese.

COVER AND BAKE for 45 minutes or until hot and bubbly. Let stand for 10 minutes before serving.

Cheesy Tuna Lasagna

Even if the sauce is homemade and not made with condensed soup, this recipe remains a pantry staple since everything is shelf or fridge stable. Use oil- or water-packed tuna, preferably types responsibly fished.

SERVES 8 TO 10

12 lasagna noodles

TUNA FILLING

2 tablespoons extra-virgin olive oil

1 red bell pepper, chopped

½ sweet onion, chopped

1 celery stalk, finely chopped

2 garlic cloves, minced

¼ teaspoon fine sea salt

¼ teaspoon freshly ground black pepper

3 (6-ounce) cans tuna, drained

2 cups frozen peas

CHEESE SAUCE

2 teaspoons butter

3 tablespoons all-purpose flour

2 cups vegetable or chicken broth

1 cup whole milk or half and half

1 cup (4 ounces) shredded cheddar cheese

1 cup (4 ounces) shredded Pepper Jack cheese

1 cup panko breadcrumbs or crushed butter crackers

½ cup (2 ounces) shredded Pepper Jack cheese

2 teaspoons extra-virgin olive oil

PREHEAT THE OVEN to 375°F. Lightly grease a 13 x 9-inch baking dish.

COOK THE LASAGNA NOODLES in boiling salted water according to the package directions. Drain, then rinse in cool water.

MAKE THE TUNA FILLING: Heat the oil in a large skillet over medium-high heat. Add the bell pepper, onion, celery, garlic, salt, and pepper. Cook, stirring frequently, for 5 to 7 minutes until the vegetables are tender. Stir in the tuna and peas.

MAKE THE CHEESE SAUCE: Melt the butter in a large skillet over medium-high heat. Whisk in the flour and cook, stirring constantly, for 1 minute. Whisk in the broth and milk and cook, stirring frequently, for 5 minutes or until the mixture thickens. Add the cheddar and Pepper Jack cheeses, stirring until smooth.

ASSEMBLE: Spread ¾ cup of the cheese sauce in the bottom of the prepared baking dish. Top with 4 noodles. Top with one-third of the tuna filling and one third of the remaining sauce. Repeat twice with remaining noodles, tuna, and sauce.

COMBINE THE PANKO, Pepper Jack, and oil in a small bowl. Sprinkle evenly over the lasagna.

COVER AND BAKE for 30 minutes. Uncover and bake for 30 minutes more or until golden brown and bubbly. Let stand for 10 minutes before serving.

SEAFOOD

Tuna & Smoky
Red Pepper Sauce Lasagna

You'll find a variety of canned tuna on the shelves, and it gets confusing. It doesn't really matter if you choose oil- or water-packed in this recipe, but I prefer the flavor of tuna packed in olive oil. I usually buy light tuna. That doesn't mean less calories or fat but rather smaller species of tuna such as skipjack. I encourage buying sustainable brands, often labeled "pole and line caught," to avoid bycatch.

SERVES 4

SMOKY RED PEPPER SAUCE

3 roasted red bell peppers, fresh roasted or jarred, drained well

2 tablespoons tomato paste

1 small garlic clove, minced

1 tablespoon extra-virgin olive oil

1 teaspoon smoked paprika

1 teaspoon Italian seasoning

½ teaspoon fine sea salt

¼ teaspoon freshly ground black pepper

Pinch sugar

ARUGULA-RICOTTA FILLING

1 (15-ounce) container ricotta cheese

1 large egg

1 teaspoon lemon zest

1 tablespoon fresh lemon juice

¼ teaspoon fine sea salt

½ (5-ounce) container fresh baby arugula, coarsely chopped

2 (6-ounce) cans tuna, drained

4 oven-ready lasagna noodles

1 cup (4 ounces) shredded mozzarella cheese

PREHEAT THE OVEN to 350°F. Lightly grease an 8 x 8-inch baking dish.

MAKE THE SMOKY RED PEPPER SAUCE: Combine the roasted peppers, tomato paste, garlic, olive oil, paprika, Italian seasoning, salt, pepper, and sugar in a blender or food processor. Pulse until well blended.

MAKE THE ARUGULA-RICOTTA FILLING: Combine the ricotta, egg, lemon zest and juice, and salt. Stir in the arugula.

ASSEMBLE: Spread ½ cup of the pepper sauce in the bottom of the prepared baking dish. Top with 2 noodles. Spread with half of the ricotta filling, half of the tuna, and half of the remaining pepper sauce. Repeat with the remaining noodles, ricotta filling, tuna, and sauce. Sprinkle with mozzarella cheese.

COVER AND BAKE for 40 minutes. Let stand for 10 minutes before serving.

DESSERT

Apple Pie Lasagna

The nutty-oat topping adds a bit of crunch and flavor, but it also protects the apples and noodles from drying out while baking. Be sure to use traditional boiled noodles since the filling isn't juicy enough to cook oven-ready ones. There's a reason for the odd number of noodles—traditional noodles are longer than the pan. Cut the excess parts of the noodles and piece them together to form another row.

~~~~~~~~~~~~~~~ **SERVES 6** ~~~~~~~~~~~~~~~

5 lasagna noodles

APPLE FILLING

½ cup sugar

¼ cup firmly packed light brown sugar

1½ tablespoons cornstarch

½ teaspoon ground cinnamon

½ teaspoon ground nutmeg

½ teaspoon freshly grated lemon zest

2 teaspoons fresh lemon juice

4 Granny Smith, Honeycrisp, or other baking apple (about 2 pounds)

OAT TOPPING

½ cup old-fashioned or quick oats

¼ cup all-purpose flour

¼ cup firmly packed light brown sugar

½ teaspoon ground cinnamon

¼ cup chopped pecans

4 tablespoons melted unsalted butter

PREHEAT THE OVEN to 350°F. Lightly grease an 8 x 8-inch or 9 x 9-inch baking dish.

COOK THE LASAGNA NOODLES in boiling salted water for 8 minutes until tender. Drain, then rinse with cool water.

MAKE THE APPLE FILLING: Combine the sugar, brown sugar, cornstarch, cinnamon, nutmeg, and lemon zest and juice in a large bowl. Stir until well blended. Peel, core, and thinly slice the apples. Add the apples to the sugar mixture, stirring until well blended. Set aside.

MAKE THE OAT TOPPING: Combine the oats, flour, brown sugar, cinnamon, and pecans in a medium bowl. Add the butter, stirring until well blended.

ASSEMBLE: Arrange 2½ noodles on the bottom of the prepared baking dish, cutting to fit the dish. Top with half of the apple mixture. Top with the remaining 2½ noodles and apple mixture. Drizzle any liquid left in the bowl over the apples. Sprinkle evenly with the oat topping.

BAKE for 45 to 55 minutes until the apples are tender and the topping is golden brown. Cover with foil after 30 minutes if the top is getting too dark. Serve warm or chilled (with ice cream!).

DESSERT

Blackberry-Peach Sweet Lasagna

For most of the year, I prefer nectarines over peaches because I like the color of the skin in recipes. (Okay, I admit I don't love peeling off-season fruit.) But it's a whole other game in summer when I've got a basket of ripe and juicy local peaches. To make it easy, cut a small x on the bottom of each peach with a sharp paring knife. Drop them into boiling water for thirty seconds to a minute. Remove with a slotted spoon, drop into a bowl of ice water, and let stand until the peaches are cool enough to handle. Drain and slip off the skins. While you've got hot boiling water, cook the pasta noodles immediately after.

SERVES 8

8 lasagna noodles

PEACH-BLACKBERRY FILLING

2 tablespoons butter

6 peaches or nectarines, peeled and sliced

¼ cup firmly packed light brown sugar

3 tablespoons sugar

2 tablespoons cornstarch

2 teaspoons fresh lemon juice

½ teaspoon ground cinnamon

Pinch salt

SWEET RICOTTA FILLING

1 (15-ounce) container ricotta cheese

1 (8-ounce) container mascarpone cheese

¾ cup sugar

2 teaspoons vanilla extract

1 large egg

1 (12-ounce) container fresh blackberries

PREHEAT THE OVEN to 375°F. Butter a 9 x 9-inch baking dish.

COOK THE LASAGNA NOODLES in boiling salted water according to the package directions. Drain, then rinse in cool water.

PREPARE THE PEACH-BLACKBERRY FILLING: Melt the butter in a large skillet over medium heat. Add the peaches and cook, tossing gently, for 2 minutes. Combine the brown sugar, sugar, cornstarch, lemon juice, cinnamon, and salt in a bowl. Sprinkle onto the fruit mixture. Cook, stirring frequently, for 5 minutes or until the mixture is thickened and the fruit is tender but not broken up or mushy. (Note: If your peaches or nectarines are very ripe and soft, there may be no need to cook the mixture since the fruit is already tender. Just combine in a large bowl.)

PREPARE THE SWEET RICOTTA FILLING: Combine the ricotta, mascarpone, sugar, vanilla, and egg in a bowl.

ASSEMBLE: Arrange 4 noodles in the bottom of the prepared dish, cutting to fit the pan. Top with half of the ricotta filling and half of the peach filling. Arrange half of the blackberries on top. Repeat with the remaining noodles, ricotta, peaches, and blackberries.

BAKE for 45 minutes or until hot and bubbly. Cool slightly or refrigerate before serving.

Berry & Cream Cheese Layered Dessert

This variation of strawberry shortcake can be made ahead of time since the cream cheese and sugar stabilize the heavy cream while adding richness and flavor. If your strawberries are very tart, toss all the slices in two tablespoons of sugar and let stand about twenty minutes. Take it up a notch by substituting orange liqueur for the fresh lemon juice.

SERVES 6 TO 8

CREAM CHEESE FILLING

- 1 (8-ounce) package cream cheese, softened
- ½ cup sour cream
- ½ cup sugar
- 2 tablespoons fresh lemon juice
- 1 teaspoon vanilla extract
- ½ cup heavy cream

- 1 (16-ounce) package frozen loaf pound cake
- 1 (16-ounce) container strawberries, sliced
- 1 cup fresh or frozen and thawed blueberries
- 1 tablespoon fresh mint leaves
- 1 teaspoon powdered sugar

MAKE THE CREAM CHEESE FILLING: Beat the cream cheese, sour cream, and sugar in a large bowl with an electric mixer until smooth. Add the lemon juice and vanilla, beating until well blended. Transfer to a bowl. Beat the heavy cream with an electric mixer until soft peaks form. Gently fold into the cream cheese mixture.

SLICE THE POUND CAKE in half lengthwise (it doesn't have to be thawed). Then slice each long plank in half lengthwise again to create four ¼-inch-thick planks.

ASSEMBLE: Butter a 9 x 9-inch baking pan. Arrange half of the pound cake in the bottom of the pan, cutting pieces to create an even layer. Spoon half of the cream cheese mixture over the pound cake and top with half of the strawberries and half of the blueberries. Repeat with the remaining pound cake, cream cheese mixture, and fruit. Cover and refrigerate until ready to serve.

GARNISH WITH FRESH MINT and sprinkle lightly with powdered sugar, if desired.

DESSERT

Spiced Pumpkin Lasagna

There's enough liquid in the pumpkin custard mixture to use oven-ready lasagna noodles. After forty-five minutes of bake time, pull aside the foil and insert a knife to make sure the noodles are tender. If not, cover again and continue to bake for five additional minutes.

~~~~~~~~~~~~~~~~ **SERVES 9** ~~~~~~~~~~~~~~~~

PUMPKIN FILLING

½ cup sugar

⅓ cup lightly packed light brown sugar

1½ teaspoons ground cinnamon

¾ teaspoon ground ginger

½ teaspoon fine sea salt

¼ teaspoon ground cloves

¼ teaspoon ground nutmeg

3 large eggs

1 (15-ounce) can pumpkin puree

1 cup whole milk

1 teaspoon vanilla extract

RICOTTA FILLING

1 (15-ounce) container ricotta cheese

1 large egg

6 to 8 oven-ready lasagna noodles

Sweetened whipped cream (optional)

PREHEAT OVEN TO 375°F. Lightly grease a 9 x 9-inch baking dish.

MAKE THE PUMPKIN FILLING: Whisk together the sugar, brown sugar, cinnamon, ginger, salt, cloves, and nutmeg in a small bowl. Beat the eggs in a large bowl. Stir in the pumpkin and spiced sugar mixture. Whisk in the milk and vanilla extract.

MAKE THE RICOTTA FILLING: Stir together the ricotta and egg in a small bowl.

ASSEMBLE: Spread 1 cup of the pumpkin mixture in the bottom of the prepared dish. Top with 2 to 2½ noodles, breaking to fit. Dollop with one-third of the ricotta filling and one-third of the pumpkin filling. Repeat twice in this order: 2 to 2½ noodles, one-third ricotta, and one-third pumpkin.

COVER AND BAKE for 45 minutes. Uncover and cool to room temperature on a wire rack. Cover and chill for several hours or overnight until firm. Serve with sweetened whipped cream, if desired.

Tiramisu

Old tiramisu recipes may use raw egg yolks, but nowadays it's recommended to cook raw eggs to at least 160°F for food safety reasons. If you don't have a double boiler, you can make one by setting a stainless-steel bowl over a pan filled with about an inch of boiling water (don't allow the boiling water to touch the bottom of the bowl). Look for crisp Italian ladyfingers that will hold up to the soaking liquid. If you can only find the soft ones (or you can substitute slices of pound cake in a pinch), place them in the pan, then brush lightly with the coffee mixture, taking care not to use so much that the cookies dissolve.

~~~~~~~~~~ **SERVES 8** ~~~~~~~~~~

6 egg yolks

¾ cup sugar

2 (8-ounce) containers mascarpone cheese, at room temperature

1 cup heavy cream

1 cup espresso or strong coffee, at room temperature

½ cup coffee-flavored liqueur or rum (optional)

1 (7-ounce) package crisp ladyfinger cookies

1 tablespoon unsweetened or bittersweet cocoa powder

WHISK TOGETHER the egg yolks and sugar in the top of a double boiler over medium heat. Whisk constantly for 10 minutes or until the mixture reaches 160°F. Remove from the heat and let cool for about 10 minutes. Add the mascarpone cheese to the egg yolk mixture, stirring until smooth and well blended. Cool to room temperature.

BEAT THE HEAVY CREAM with an electric mixer until stiff peaks form. Fold the whipped cream into the mascarpone mixture.

POUR THE ESPRESSO AND COFFEE LIQUEUR, if using, into a shallow bowl. Dip half the ladyfingers, one at a time, into the coffee mixture until just soaked but not soggy. Arrange the soaked ladyfingers in the bottom of a 9-inch-square baking dish.

SPOON HALF THE MASCARPONE FILLING over the ladyfingers. Dip the remaining half of the ladyfingers in the remaining coffee mixture and arrange over the filling. Spoon the remaining mascarpone filling over the ladyfingers. Refrigerate or freeze for at least 4 to 6 hours. Sprinkle evenly with the cocoa powder before serving. If frozen, thaw servings for a few minutes before serving.

Chocolate Peanut Butter Layered Dessert

This simple and oh-so-rich layered dessert features a fantastic flavor combo—chocolate and peanut butter! If you like a bit more texture, use chunky peanut butter. You can even use a chocolate hazelnut spread for another variation.

~~~~~~~~~~ **SERVES 12** ~~~~~~~~~~

1½ cups crushed chocolate graham crackers (1 sleeve) or thin chocolate cookies

4 tablespoons unsalted butter, melted

1½ cups heavy cream

1 (8-ounce) package cream cheese, softened

⅔ cup creamy peanut butter

½ cup powdered sugar

1 teaspoon vanilla extract

4 ounces semisweet or sweet dark chocolate, chopped

Optional garnishes: whipped cream, chocolate curls, or chopped peanut butter cups

LINE AN 8 X 8-INCH BAKING DISH with nonstick foil.

COMBINE THE CRUSHED CRACKERS and melted butter in a bowl; set aside.

BEAT 1 CUP OF THE HEAVY CREAM at medium speed with an electric mixer until soft peaks form. Transfer to another bowl and set aside.

BEAT THE CREAM CHEESE, peanut butter, powdered sugar, and vanilla until creamy. In batches, gently fold into the whipped cream.

ASSEMBLE: Line the bottom of the baking dish with half of the crushed graham crackers. Spoon half of the peanut butter mixture over the graham cracker layer. Repeat with the remaining crushed graham crackers and peanut butter mixture. Cover with plastic wrap and place in the freezer for several hours until firm.

HEAT THE REMAINING ½ CUP CREAM in the microwave for 30 seconds. Stir in the chocolate and continue to heat at 15-second increments until melted. Pour the chocolate mixture over the top of the dessert. Freeze until firm.

LIFT OUT OF THE BAKING DISH and peel foil away before cutting. Serve with whipped cream, chocolate curls, or chopped peanut butter cups, if desired.

Layered Chocolate Éclair Dessert

You may see some shortcut versions of this dessert using packaged vanilla pudding. You can substitute two boxes, but try the homemade vanilla pudding below. If you want to go upscale, scrape the seeds of a vanilla bean into the sugar mixture before preparing and skip the extract. I included two options to layer with the vanilla pudding: graham crackers or pound cake—your choice! There will be extra graham crackers, but I called for the entire box since you'll only have a few left over.

~~~~~~~~~~ **SERVES 6** *~~~~~~~~~~*

VANILLA PUDDING

- 5 large egg yolks
- ⅔ cup sugar
- ¼ cup cornstarch
- ⅛ teaspoon fine salt
- 2½ cups whole milk or half and half
- 3 tablespoons unsalted butter, cut into pieces
- 1 tablespoon vanilla extract

- 1 (16-ounce) frozen pound cake or 1 (14.4-ounce) box graham crackers

CHOCOLATE GANACHE TOPPING

- ½ cup heavy cream
- 1 tablespoon light corn syrup
- 4 ounces semisweet or sweet dark chocolate

MAKE THE VANILLA PUDDING: Whisk together the egg yolks in a small bowl. Combine the sugar, cornstarch, and salt in a saucepan. Gradually whisk in the milk. Bring to a boil over medium heat, stirring constantly. Boil for 1 minute, stirring constantly, until the mixture thickens. Remove the pan from the heat. Slowly stir about 1 cup of the hot milk mixture into the eggs to loosen up them up. Pour the egg-milk mixture back into the saucepan. Return the pan to the heat and bring to a boil over medium. Boil for 1 minute, stirring constantly. Remove from the heat and stir in the butter and vanilla. Transfer to a bowl, cover the surface with plastic wrap, and refrigerate until completely cold.

ASSEMBLE FOR POUND CAKE LAYERS: Slice the pound cake in half lengthwise (it doesn't have to be thawed). Slice each long plank in half lengthwise again to create four ¼-inch-thick planks. Butter a 9 x 9-inch baking dish. Arrange half of the pound cake in the bottom of the pan, cutting pieces to create an even layer. Spoon half of the vanilla pudding on top. Arrange the remaining pound cake on top and spread with the remaining pudding.

ASSEMBLE FOR GRAHAM CRACKER LAYERS: Butter a 9 x 9-inch baking dish. Arrange a layer of graham crackers on the bottom. Spoon half of the pudding over the crackers. Repeat with another layer of graham crackers and the remaining half of pudding. Top with a layer of graham crackers.

MAKE THE CHOCOLATE GANACHE TOPPING: Combine the heavy cream and corn syrup in a glass measuring cup. Microwave in 30-second increments until hot. Add the chocolate and let stand 5 minutes, then stir until well blended. Microwave for 15-second increments if the chocolate did not completely melt. Cool slightly. Spread the chocolate over the top of the dessert. Cover and chill about 3 hours or until set.

Brownie–Chocolate Chip Layered Bars

The caramel layer holds up better if you wait until they are cool before cutting into pieces. However, if you love the idea of warm, gooey caramel drooling from the cookies onto your plate, then scoop out samples a few minutes out of the oven.

~~~~~~~~~~ **SERVES 12** ~~~~~~~~~~

BROWNIE LAYER

½ **cup (1 stick) unsalted butter, softened**

¾ **cup granulated sugar**

¼ **cup light brown sugar**

2 **large eggs**

1 **teaspoon vanilla extract**

⅔ **cup unsweetened cocoa powder**

½ **cup all-purpose flour**

¼ **teaspoon fine sea salt**

CHOCOLATE CHIP COOKIE LAYER

½ **cup (1 stick) unsalted butter, softened**

½ **cup granulated sugar**

½ **cup firmly packed light brown sugar**

1 **large egg**

1 **teaspoon vanilla extract**

1½ **cups all-purpose flour**

¾ **teaspoon baking soda**

¼ **teaspoon fine sea salt**

¾ **cup semisweet chocolate chips**

15 **to 20 small soft caramels**

PREHEAT THE OVEN to 325°F. Line an 8 x 8-inch baking pan with nonstick foil.

MAKE THE BROWNIE LAYER: Beat the butter, sugar, and brown sugar at medium speed with an electric mixer until well blended. Beat in the eggs and vanilla. Stir together the cocoa powder, flour, and salt. Add to the butter mixture by heaping tablespoons (the cocoa mixture will splash out if not added slowly), stirring until well blended. Set aside.

MAKE THE CHOCOLATE CHIP COOKIE LAYER: Beat the butter, sugar, and brown sugar at medium speed with an electric mixer until well blended. Beat in the egg and vanilla. Stir together the flour, baking soda, and salt. Add to the butter mixture, stirring until well blended. Stir in the chocolate chips.

ASSEMBLE: Spread the brownie mixture in the bottom of the prepared pan and sprinkle evenly with the caramel pieces. Drop spoonfuls of the cookie dough over the caramels, and press into an even layer.

BAKE for 30 minutes until a wooden pick inserted in the center comes out clean. Cool completely on a wire rack.

DESSERT

Espresso Crepe Cake

Each piece of this thin and lightweight layered dessert is richly flavored. Make up to three days ahead but don't top with the whipped cream or other toppings until ready to serve.

〜〜〜〜〜〜 **SERVES 12** 〜〜〜〜〜〜

3 large egg yolks

¼ cup sugar

2 cups heavy cream

1 tablespoon instant espresso granules

6 ounces bittersweet chocolate, chopped

1 teaspoon vanilla extract

1 (5-ounce) package refrigerated prepared crepes or 10 (9-inch) homemade crepes

Optional garnishes:
Sweetened whipped cream, chocolate-covered espresso beans, shaved chocolate, fresh raspberries

WHISK TOGETHER the egg yolks and sugar in a medium bowl. Heat 1 cup of the heavy cream and espresso granules in a saucepan over medium heat until hot but not boiling. Pour the hot cream into the egg yolk mixture in a slow stream, whisking until well blended.

TRANSFER THE MIXTURE back into the saucepan. Cook, stirring frequently, over medium-low heat for 10 minutes or until it reaches 160°F and the mixture is slightly thickened. Transfer to a bowl and stir in the chocolate and vanilla. Let stand until chocolate melts, stirring until smooth. Cover and refrigerate until completely chilled.

REMOVE THE ESPRESSO MIXTURE and let stand at room temperature until easy to stir. Beat the remaining 1 cup heavy cream with an electric mixture until stiff peaks form. Gradually fold the whipped cream into the chocolate-espresso mixture.

ASSEMBLE: Place a crepe on a serving plate and spread with 4 to 5 tablespoons of the espresso mousse mixture. Repeat with the remaining crepes and mousse, spreading the last bit of mousse over the top. Cover (without letting the plastic wrap touch) and refrigerate for 1 to 2 hours or until firm.

TOP THE CREPE CAKE with the whipped cream, chocolate-covered espresso beans, shaved chocolate, or raspberries, if desired.

DESSERT

171

Maple Sticky Bun Lasagna

Most homemade sticky bun recipes require yeast and an hour-plus of rising time. This recipe uses a quick dough, so you can have this sweet and spontaneous breakfast treat even when you oversleep. Buttermilk adds flavor and moistness to the quick dough, but its secret mission is using acidity to help the quick dough rise while increasing tenderness. If you don't have any buttermilk, you can thin down plain yogurt or sour cream until it has the same thickness as heavy cream. For a variation, stir two teaspoons of grated orange zest into the dough.

SERVES 8

QUICK DOUGH

4 cups all-purpose flour

2 tablespoons baking powder

2 tablespoons sugar

1 teaspoon salt

½ cup (1 stick) unsalted butter, cut into small pieces

1¼ cups buttermilk

MAPLE-CARAMEL FILLING

½ cup firmly packed light or dark brown sugar

2 teaspoons ground cinnamon

½ cup pure maple syrup

4 tablespoons unsalted butter, melted

½ teaspoon vanilla extract

1 cup chopped pecans

1 tablespoon unsalted butter, softened

1 teaspoon granulated sugar

Pinch ground cinnamon

PREHEAT THE OVEN to 350°F. Butter an 8-cup, 8 x 8-, or 9 x 9-inch baking dish.

MAKE THE QUICK DOUGH: Combine the flour, baking powder, sugar, and salt in a large bowl. Cut in butter with a pastry blender or fork until crumbly. Add the buttermilk, stirring until a thick dough forms.

MAKE THE MAPLE-CARAMEL FILLING: Stir together the brown sugar and cinnamon in a large bowl. Stir in the syrup, butter, and vanilla. Stir in the pecans.

ASSEMBLE: Divide the dough into thirds. Roll each portion on a floured surface about the size of the baking dish. Place one layer of dough in the bottom of the prepared dish. Spread half of the maple filling over the dough. Top with another layer of dough, the remaining half of the filling, and the remaining dough layer.

BRUSH THE TOP with the softened butter. Combine the sugar and cinnamon and in a small bowl and sprinkle over the top.

BAKE for 35 minutes or until golden brown and cooked through.

Spiced Baklava

This sweet dessert features dozens of thin pastry layers filled with lightly spiced nuts. I prefer the trio of mixed nuts, but you can substitute one for another as well as experimenting with pine nuts or pistachios. Use a light metal baking pan, since glass or ceramic baking dishes can overcook the baklava, making it tough and difficult to cut. Keep the baklava in the refrigerator and allow to come to room temperature before eating.

SERVES ABOUT 36

SPICED NUT FILLING

1⅓ cups slivered almonds

1⅓ cups chopped walnuts

1⅓ cups chopped pecans

2 teaspoons ground cinnamon

½ teaspoon ground nutmeg

⅛ teaspoon ground cloves

⅓ cup sugar

1 cup (2 sticks) unsalted butter

1 (16-ounce) package frozen and thawed phyllo dough

SPICED HONEY SYRUP

1 cup sugar

½ cup honey

½ cup water

2 tablespoons fresh lemon juice

⅛ teaspoon ground cinnamon

MAKE THE SPICED NUT FILLING: Combine the almonds, walnuts, pecans, cinnamon, nutmeg, and cloves in a food processor. Process until very finely chopped. Add the sugar. Pulse until mixture is finely chopped. Set aside.

MELT THE BUTTER in a small saucepan over low heat. Skim away the white foam from the top of the butter. Keep warm.

BUTTER A 13 X 9-INCH BAKING PAN. Unroll the phyllo dough and keep it covered with a lightly damp towel while assembling to prevent it from drying out and cracking. Trim the phyllo to fit the pan, if necessary.

ASSEMBLE: Place 1 sheet of phyllo in the bottom of the prepared pan. Brush with the melted butter. Top with 9 more sheets of phyllo, brushing each one with butter after being placed in the pan.

SPRINKLE ABOUT ¾ CUP OF THE NUT MIXTURE evenly over the phyllo. Top with 5 sheets of phyllo, brushing each sheet with melted butter. Repeat layering the nut mixture and 5 sheets of

buttered phyllo until all of the nut mixture is used. Top with any remaining sheets of phyllo, buttering each one as it is used.

PLACE THE BAKLAVA in the refrigerator for about 15 minutes or until firm and easy to cut. Cut the baklava all the way through into a 1½-inch-wide diamond or square pattern.

PREHEAT THE OVEN to 350°F. Bake for 45 minutes until golden brown. Place the pan on a wire rack to cool.

MAKE THE SPICED HONEY SYRUP: Combine the sugar, honey, ½ cup water, the lemon juice, and cinnamon in a saucepan over medium heat. Bring to a boil, reduce the heat to low, and simmer for 10 minutes. Cool to room temperature.

POUR THE SPICED SYRUP over top of the baklava, allowing it to seep into the cut edges. Let stand at room temperature for several hours or until the syrup has soaked into each piece. Store in the refrigerator and serve at room temperature.

DESSERT

173

Layered Almond Meringue

I used to make a meringue cake from Julia Child's 1989 book, *The Way to Cook*, as one of my favorite show-stopping desserts and followed the directions exactly as written. I must have had a lot more time and patience back then because I'm taking a lot of shortcuts these days. I admit there are still a lot of steps even in this variation, but the rich almond flavor is divine. Meringue works best on a dry day, but you can make the layers on a sunny day and freeze them until ready to assemble. It's a fantastic treat for company and holds very well in the freezer for several weeks.

--- **SERVES 12 TO 15** ---

MERINGUE LAYERS

- 1½ cups toasted sliced almonds
- 1½ cups plus 3 tablespoons sugar, divided
- 6 large egg whites
- ⅛ teaspoon fine sea salt
- ¼ teaspoon cream of tartar
- 2 teaspoons vanilla extract
- ¼ teaspoon almond extract

BUTTERCREAM FROSTING

- 1 cup granulated sugar
- 4 large egg whites
- 2 teaspoons vanilla extract
- 2 sticks (1 cup) unsalted butter, softened to room temperature

- 2 ounces semisweet or dark chocolate, melted
- 1 teaspoon almond liqueur or ⅛ teaspoon almond extract
- ¼ cup apricot jam
- 1 cup toasted almonds
- Chocolate shavings (optional)

PREHEAT THE OVEN to 250°F. Line two baking sheets with parchment paper and draw three 12 x 4-inch rectangles.

MAKE THE MERINGUE LAYERS: Combine ¾ cup almonds and ¾ cup sugar in a food processor. Pulse until the nuts are very finely ground. Transfer to a bowl and repeat with the remaining ¾ cup almonds and ¾ cup sugar.

BEAT THE EGG WHITES in a mixing bowl on slow speed until foamy. Add the salt and cream of tartar. Slowly increase the speed and beat at medium-high speed until soft peaks form. With the mixer running, gradually sprinkle in the remaining 3 tablespoons sugar. Add the vanilla and almond extracts and beat until stiff peaks form. Fold in the almond-sugar mixture with a spatula.

SPOON THE MERINGUE MIXTURE into a large piping bag or large plastic storage bag and cut a ½-inch tip. Pipe the meringue mixture evenly into the rectangles. Smooth with an offset spatula to an even thickness.

BAKE for 1 to 1½ hours, rotating the pans every 30 minutes. The meringues will be done when they are dry and can be slid loosely from the pan with a gentle push. They should remain pale. Cool completely on wire racks.

MAKE THE BUTTERCREAM FROSTING: Place the sugar in a food processor and process for 30 seconds or until fine and powdery. Transfer to a double boiler or medium metal or glass bowl placed over 1 inch of simmering water. Whisk the egg whites into the sugar. Cook, whisking occasionally, for 5 minutes. (The eggs should reach 160°F for food safety; do not heat further.) Transfer the sugar mixture into a mixing bowl. Add the vanilla extract and beat on high speed until stiff and shiny peaks form. The egg mixture should be room temperature. Beat in the butter a few pieces at a time until light and fluffy. If the mixture seems grainy, refrigerate the entire bowl for about 5 minutes to cool. Beat again until fluffy.

SPOON ½ CUP OF THE FROSTING into one bowl. Fold in the melted chocolate. Spoon another ½ cup of frosting into another bowl. Stir in the almond liqueur.

ASSEMBLE: Melt the apricot jam in a glass cup in the microwave; strain any large pieces. Brush a thin coating over the top of each meringue. Spread the almond-flavored buttercream over one of the meringues and top with a second meringue. Spread with the chocolate buttercream and top with the remaining meringue. Spread the remaining plain buttercream over the top and sides. Press the sliced almonds on the sides of the meringue cake and top with chocolate shavings, if desired.

REFRIGERATE for at least 4 hours. Cover the cake with a tent of foil or other container that will not touch the frosting. The cake may be frozen up to a month. Thaw slightly before slicing and serving.

Metric Charts

The recipes that appear in this cookbook use the standard US method for measuring liquid and dry or solid ingredients (teaspoons, tablespoons, and cups). The information on these pages is provided to help cooks outside the United States successfully use these recipes. All equivalents are approximate.

Metric Equivalents for Different Types of Ingredients

A standard cup measure of a dry or solid ingredient will vary in weight depending on the type of ingredient. A standard cup of liquid is the same volume for any type of liquid. Use the following chart when converting standard cup measures to grams (weight) or milliliters (volume).

STANDARD CUP	FINE POWDER (ex. flour)	GRAIN (ex. rice)	GRANULAR (ex. sugar)	LIQUID SOLIDS (ex. butter)	LIQUID (ex. milk)
1	140 g	150 g	190 g	200 g	240 ml
¾	105 g	113 g	143 g	150 g	180 ml
⅔	93 g	100 g	125 g	133 g	160 ml
½	70 g	75 g	95 g	100 g	120 ml
⅓	47 g	50 g	63 g	67 g	80 ml
¼	35 g	38 g	48 g	50 g	60 ml
⅛	18 g	19 g	24 g	25g	30 ml

Useful Equivalents for Dry Ingredients by Weight

(To convert ounces to grams, multiply the number of ounces by 30.)

OZ	LB	G
1 oz	¹⁄₁₆ lb	30 g
4 oz	¼ lb	120 g
8 oz	½ lb	240 g
12 oz	¾ lb	360 g
16 oz	1 lb	480 g

Useful Equivalents for Length

(To convert inches to centimeters, multiply the number of inches by 2.5.)

IN	FT	YD	CM	M
1 in			2.5 cm	
6 in	½ ft		15 cm	
12 in	1 ft		30 cm	
36 in	3 ft	1 yd	90 cm	
40 in			100 cm	1 m

Useful Equivalents for Liquid Ingredients by Volume

TSP	TBSP	CUPS	FL OZ	ML	L
¼ tsp				1 ml	
½ tsp				2 ml	
1 tsp				5 ml	
3 tsp	1 Tbsp		½ fl oz	15 ml	
	2 Tbsp	⅛ cup	1 fl oz	30 ml	
	4 Tbsp	¼ cup	2 fl oz	60 ml	
	5⅓ Tbsp	⅓ cup	3 fl oz	80 ml	
	8 Tbsp	½ cup	4 fl oz	120 ml	
	10⅔ Tbsp	⅔ cup	5 fl oz	160 ml	
	12 Tbsp	¾ cup	6 fl oz	180 ml	
	16 Tbsp	1 cup	8 fl oz	240 ml	
	1 pt	2 cups	16 fl oz	480 ml	
	1 qt	4 cups	32 fl oz	960 ml	
			33 fl oz	1000 ml	1 l

Useful Equivalents for Cooking/Oven Temperatures

	FAHRENHEIT	CELSIUS	GAS MARK
FREEZE WATER	32°F	0°C	
ROOM TEMPERATURE	68°F	20°C	
BOIL WATER	212°F	100°C	
	325°F	160°C	3
	350°F	180°C	4
	375°F	190°C	5
	400°F	200°C	6
	425°F	220°C	7
	450°F	230°C	8
BROIL			Grill

ACKNOWLEDGMENTS

Writing a comfort-food cookbook is a joy.

Developing and tasting comfort food in the middle of a period of high anxiety was therapy. I started this book in the early days of the COVID-19 stay-at-home orders. And while freelancer writers are no stranger to days spent emotionally quarantining before a deadline, a self-imposed lockdown is voluntary. Losing the basic freedom of movement in society is humbling, thought-provoking, and frightening. It's no wonder people turned to their kitchens—cooking and baking for a sense of well-being.

Testing this book required countless visits to grocery stores with frustrating delays in finding even the simplest ingredients, such as cheese, ground beef, and chicken. All the while, employees did their best to keep shelves stocked with what was available and create the safest possible environment in which to shop. My first, most sincere thanks goes to all the people working to ensure we can put food on our tables. You are much appreciated.

The upside to developing and testing a book that serves 766 (that's for the whole book!) is that there are plenty of samples I can pass along to family and neighbors. In light of social distancing, I developed a texting strategy with the neighborhood tasters. After a message indicating what lasagnas I made that day, I put wrapped samples on my front porch for a safe-distance pick up. (Yes, I'll admit it here: I was a bit relieved that I didn't have to invite them inside, so there was no need to fret about the dishes or unswept floors!) So, many thanks for the interest and input from my dear neighbors: Vicki Fuog, Paige Geier, and Sharon Mannion.

Few people benefit or suffer from a cookbook project like the family! It was a great luxury to test a book that my carnivore, vegetarian, and pescatarian family members each had a chance to enjoy. Special thanks to my daughter Corinne. While other high-school kids were probably watching their screens, she stepped up to be my culinary assistant in the days before online learning was implemented. She was even inspired to create a few of her own lasagna recipes. Hugs and love to my husband, Dit, and daughter, Emily, who did their part in tasting—I'm so grateful for their support.

Index

T

U

V

ABOUT
THE AUTHOR

JULIA RUTLAND is a Washington, DC–area writer and recipe developer whose work appears regularly in publications and websites such as *Southern Living* magazine, *Coastal Living* magazine, and Weight Watchers books. She is the author of *Discover Dinnertime, The Campfire Foodie Cookbook, On a Stick Cookbook, Blueberries: 50 Tried and True Recipes, Squash: 50 Tried and True Recipes, Apples: 50 Tried and True Recipes,* and *Foil Pack Dinners.* Julia lives in the DC wine country town of Hillsboro, Virginia, with her husband, two daughters, and many furred and feathered friends.